STAR WARS

CLONE WARS

ADVENTURES

VOLUME 10

Designer
Darin Fabrick

Assistant Editor
Dave Marshall

Editor
Jeremy Barlow

Publisher
Mike Richardson

Special thanks to Elaine Mederer, Jann Moorhead, David Anderman,
Leland Chee, Sue Rostoni, and Carol Roeder at Lucas Licensing

The events in these stories take place
sometime during the Clone Wars.

Published by
Dark Horse Books
A division of Dark Horse Comics, Inc.
10956 SE Main Street
Milwaukie, OR 97222

darkhorse.com
starwars.com

To find a comics shop in your area, call the
Comic Shop Locator Service toll-free at 1-888-266-4226

First edition: December 2007
ISBN: 978-1-59307-878-2

1 3 5 7 9 10 8 6 4 2
Printed in China

STAR WARS: CLONE WARS ADVENTURES VOLUME 10

STAR WARS®
CLONE WARS
ADVENTURES
VOLUME 10

GRADUATION DAY
script Chris Avellone
art Stewart McKenny
colors Ronda Pattison

THUNDER ROAD
script and art The Fillbach Brothers
colors Pamela Rambo

CHAIN OF COMMAND
script Jason Hall
art Ethen Beavers
colors Dan Jackson

WAITING
script and art The Fillbach Brothers
colors Tony Avina

lettering
Michael Heisler

cover
The Fillbach Brothers and Dan Jackson

Dark Horse Books®

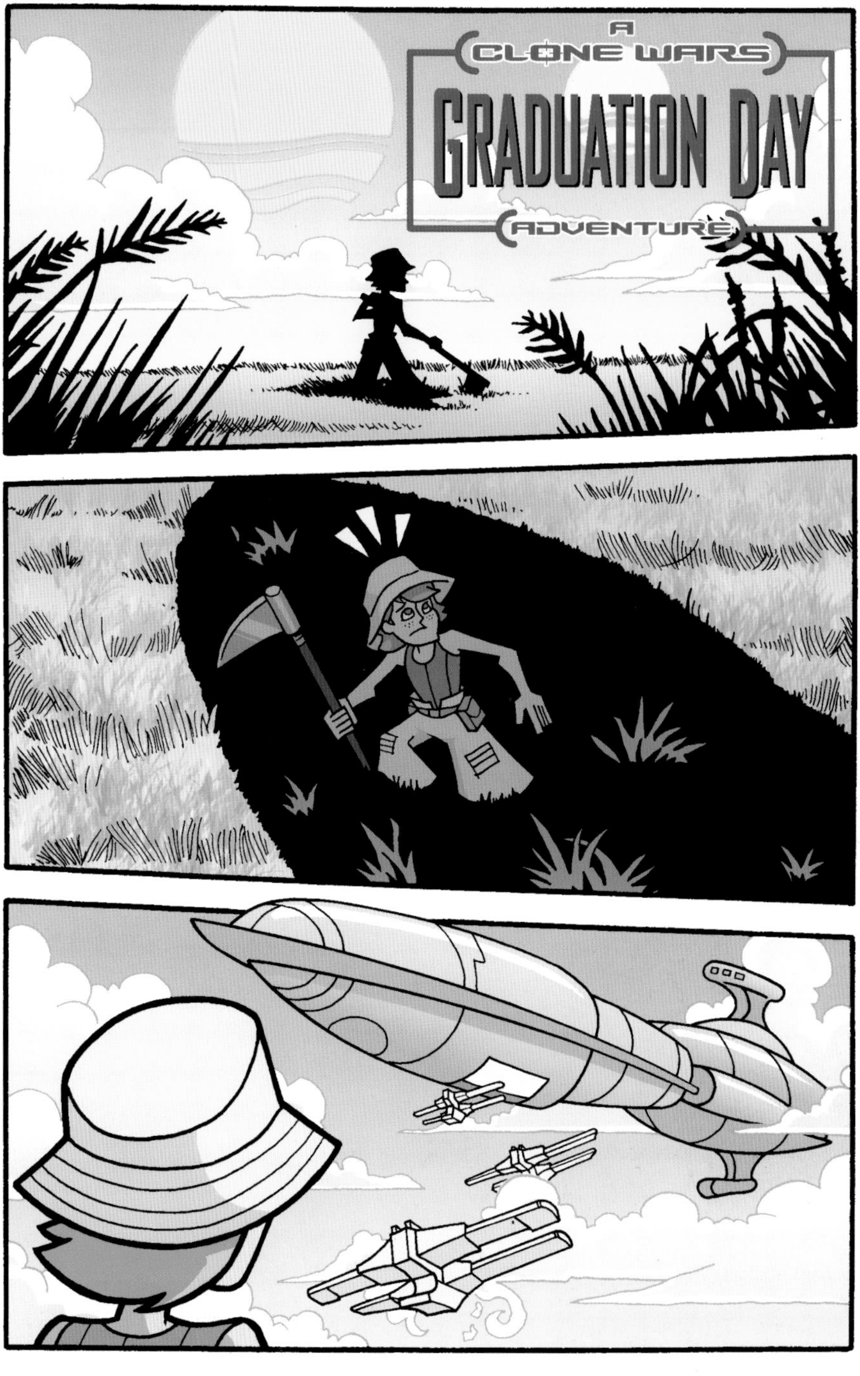
A
CLONE WARS
GRADUATION DAY
ADVENTURE

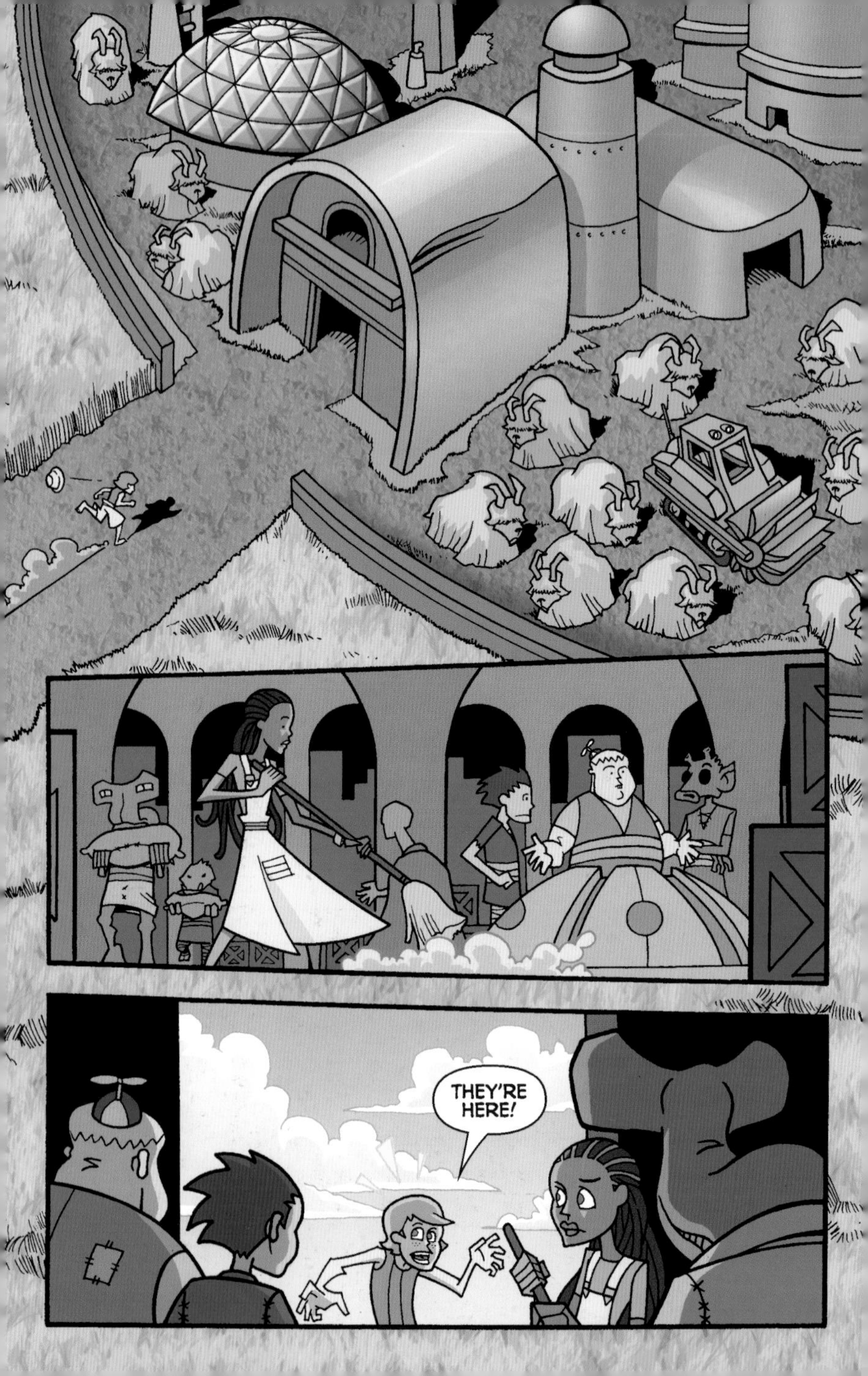
THEY'RE HERE!

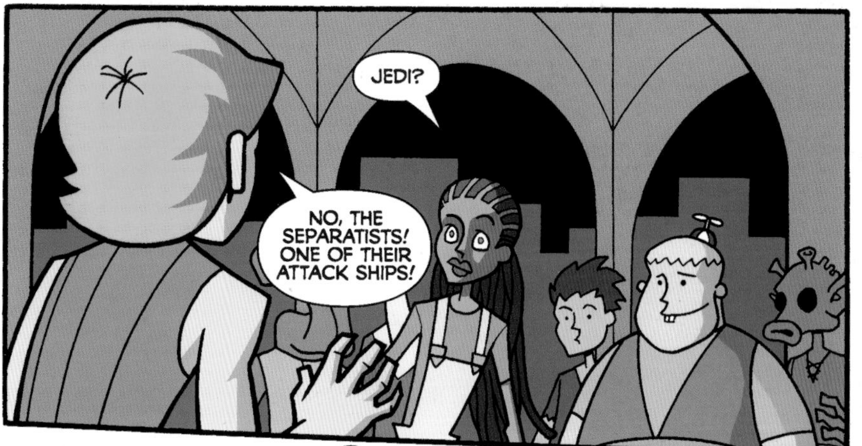
JEDI?
NO, THE SEPARATISTS! ONE OF THEIR ATTACK SHIPS!

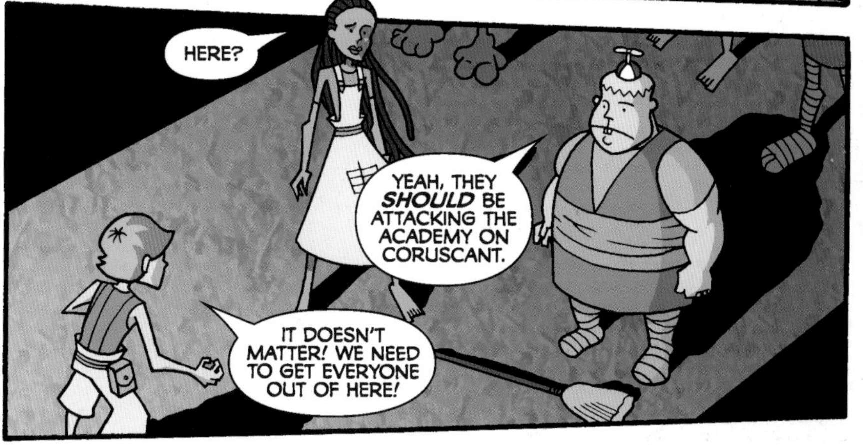
HERE?
YEAH, THEY SHOULD BE ATTACKING THE ACADEMY ON CORUSCANT.
IT DOESN'T MATTER! WE NEED TO GET EVERYONE OUT OF HERE!

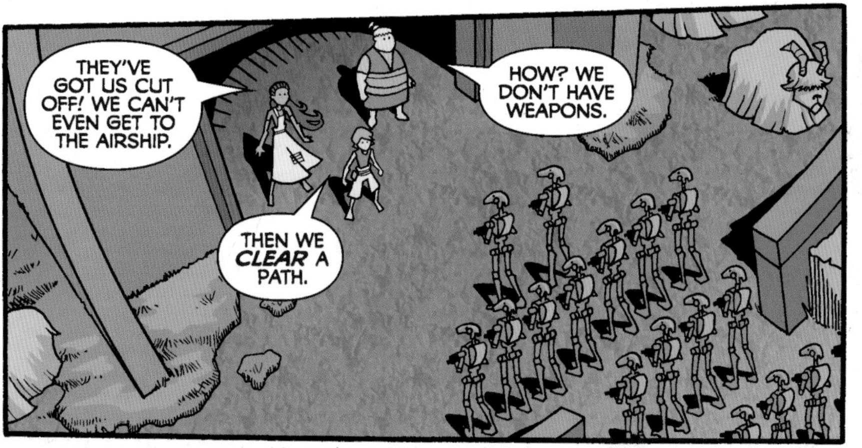
THEY'VE GOT US CUT OFF! WE CAN'T EVEN GET TO THE AIRSHIP.
HOW? WE DON'T HAVE WEAPONS.
THEN WE CLEAR A PATH.

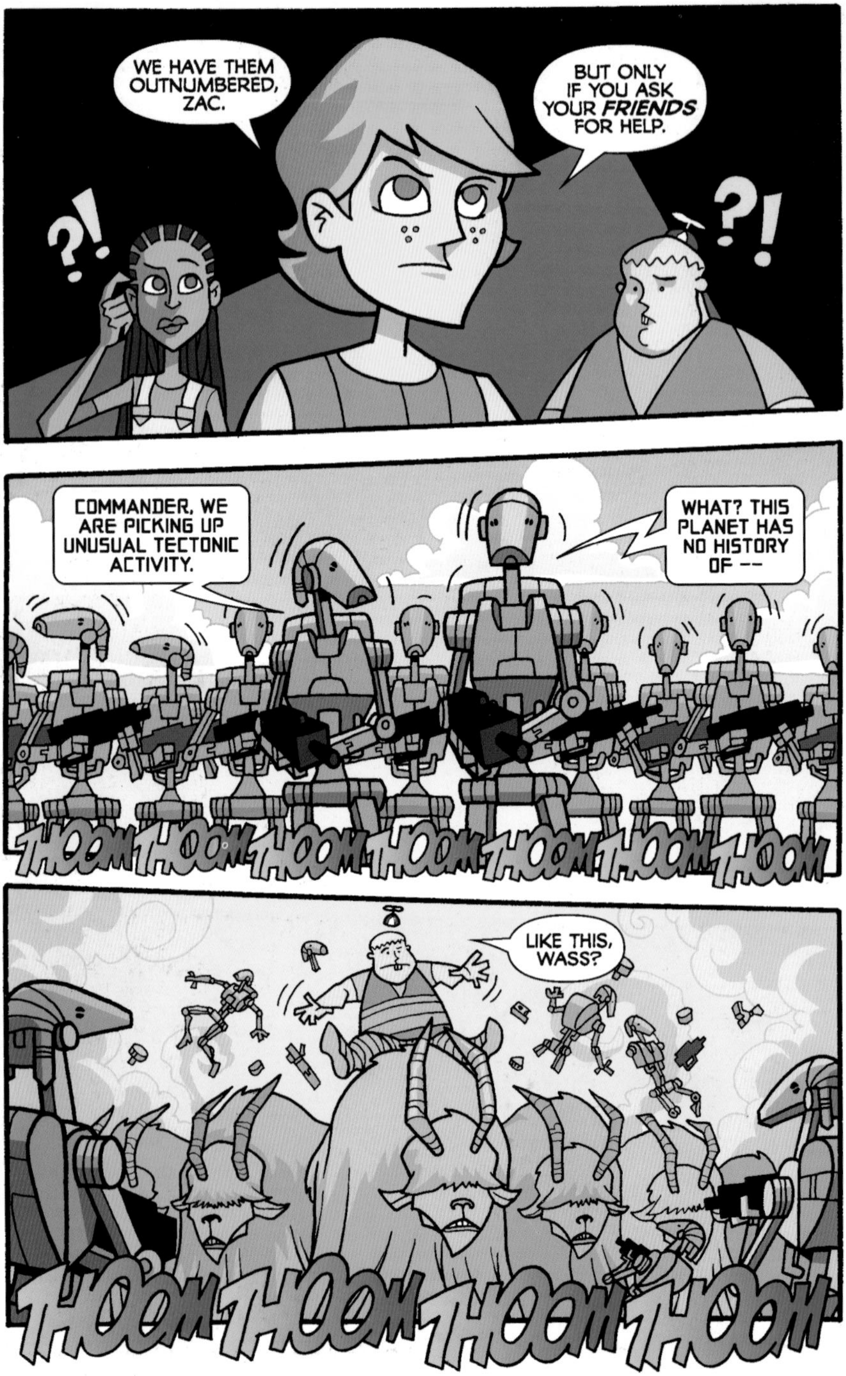
WE HAVE THEM OUTNUMBERED, ZAC.
BUT ONLY IF YOU ASK YOUR *FRIENDS* FOR HELP.
?!
?!
COMMANDER, WE ARE PICKING UP UNUSUAL TECTONIC ACTIVITY.
WHAT? THIS PLANET HAS NO HISTORY OF --
THOOM THOOM THOOM THOOM THOOM THOOM THOOM
LIKE THIS, WASS?
THOOM THOOM THOOM THOOM

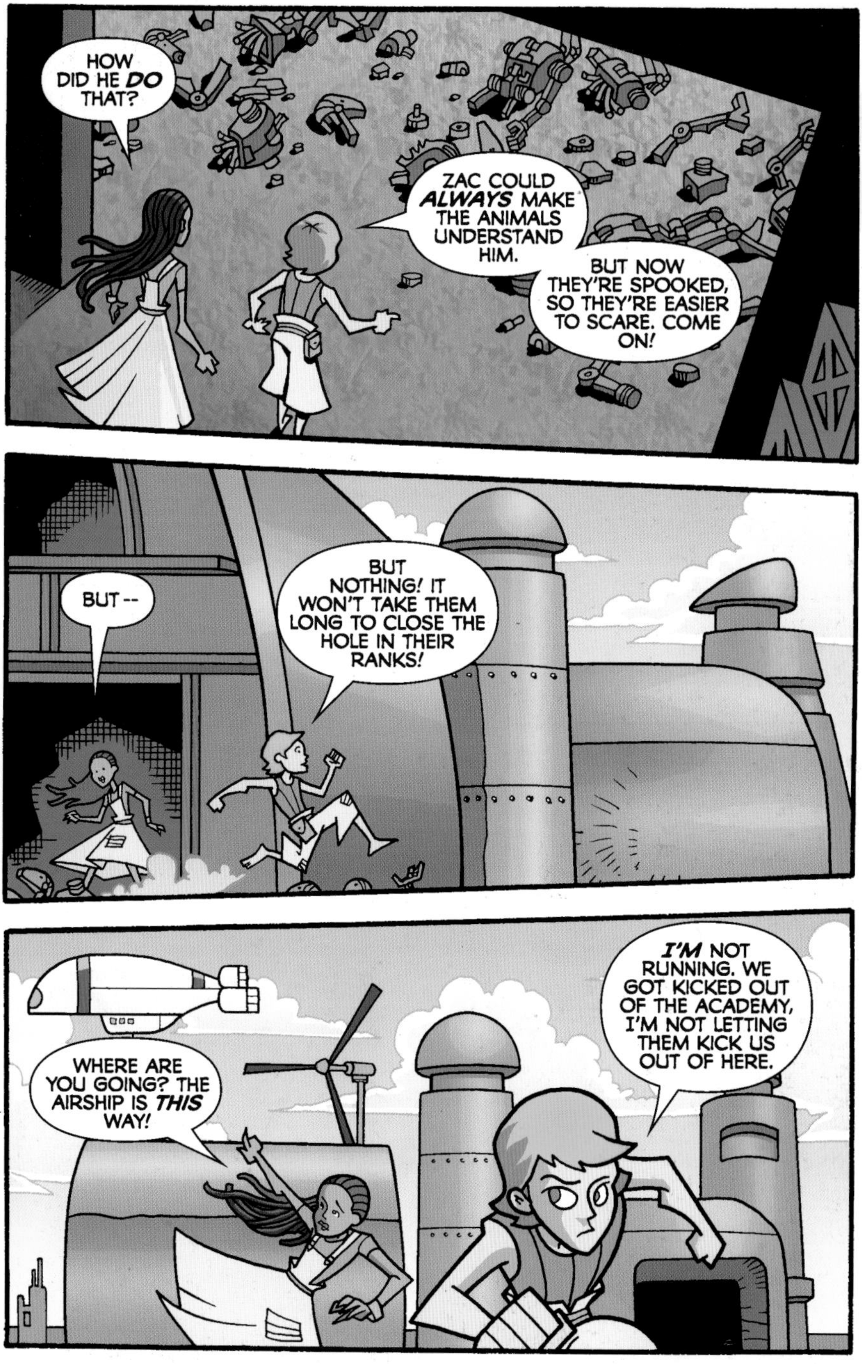
HOW DID HE *DO* THAT?
ZAC COULD *ALWAYS* MAKE THE ANIMALS UNDERSTAND HIM.
BUT NOW THEY'RE SPOOKED, SO THEY'RE EASIER TO SCARE. COME ON!
BUT --
BUT NOTHING! IT WON'T TAKE THEM LONG TO CLOSE THE HOLE IN THEIR RANKS!
WHERE ARE YOU GOING? THE AIRSHIP IS *THIS* WAY!
I'M NOT RUNNING. WE GOT KICKED OUT OF THE ACADEMY, I'M NOT LETTING THEM KICK US OUT OF HERE.

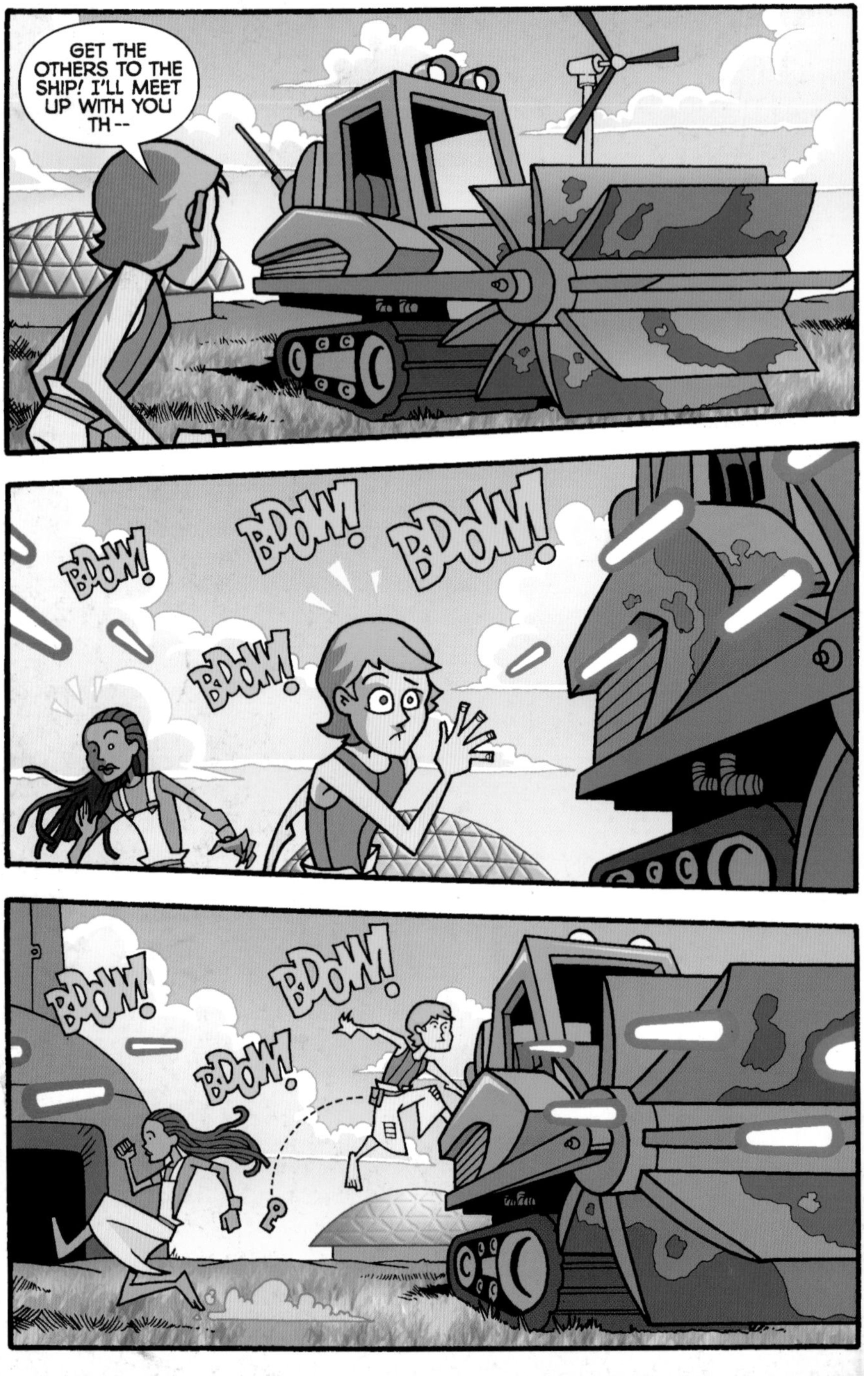
GET THE OTHERS TO THE SHIP! I'LL MEET UP WITH YOU TH--
BDOOM!
BDOOM!
BDOOM!
BDOOM!
BDOOM!
BDOOM!
BDOOM!

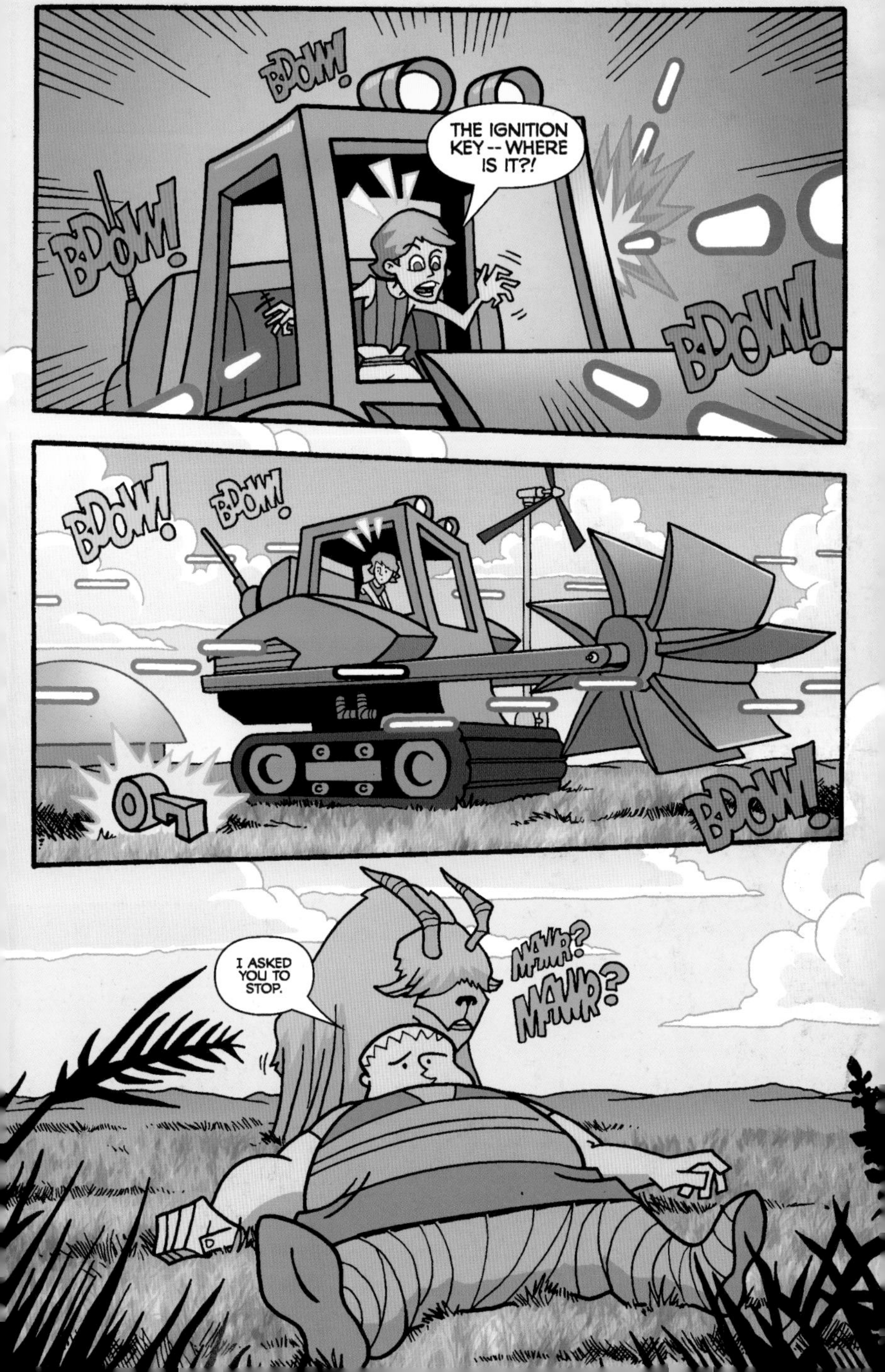
B-DOW!
THE IGNITION KEY -- WHERE IS IT?!
B-DOW!
B-DOW!
B-DOW!
B-DOW!
B-DOW!
I ASKED YOU TO STOP.
MAWR?
MAWR?

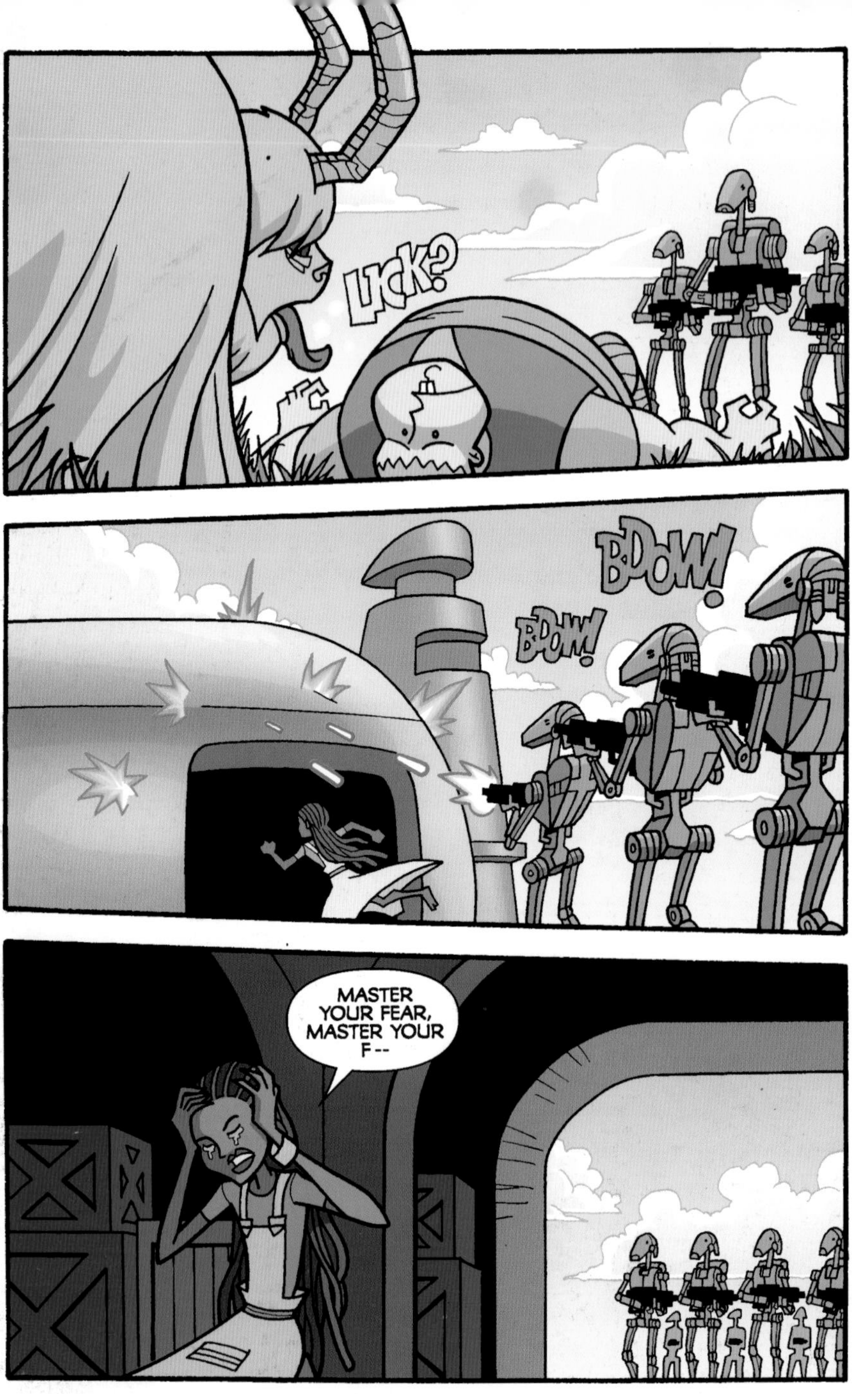
LICK?
BDOW!
BDOW!
MASTER YOUR FEAR, MASTER YOUR F--

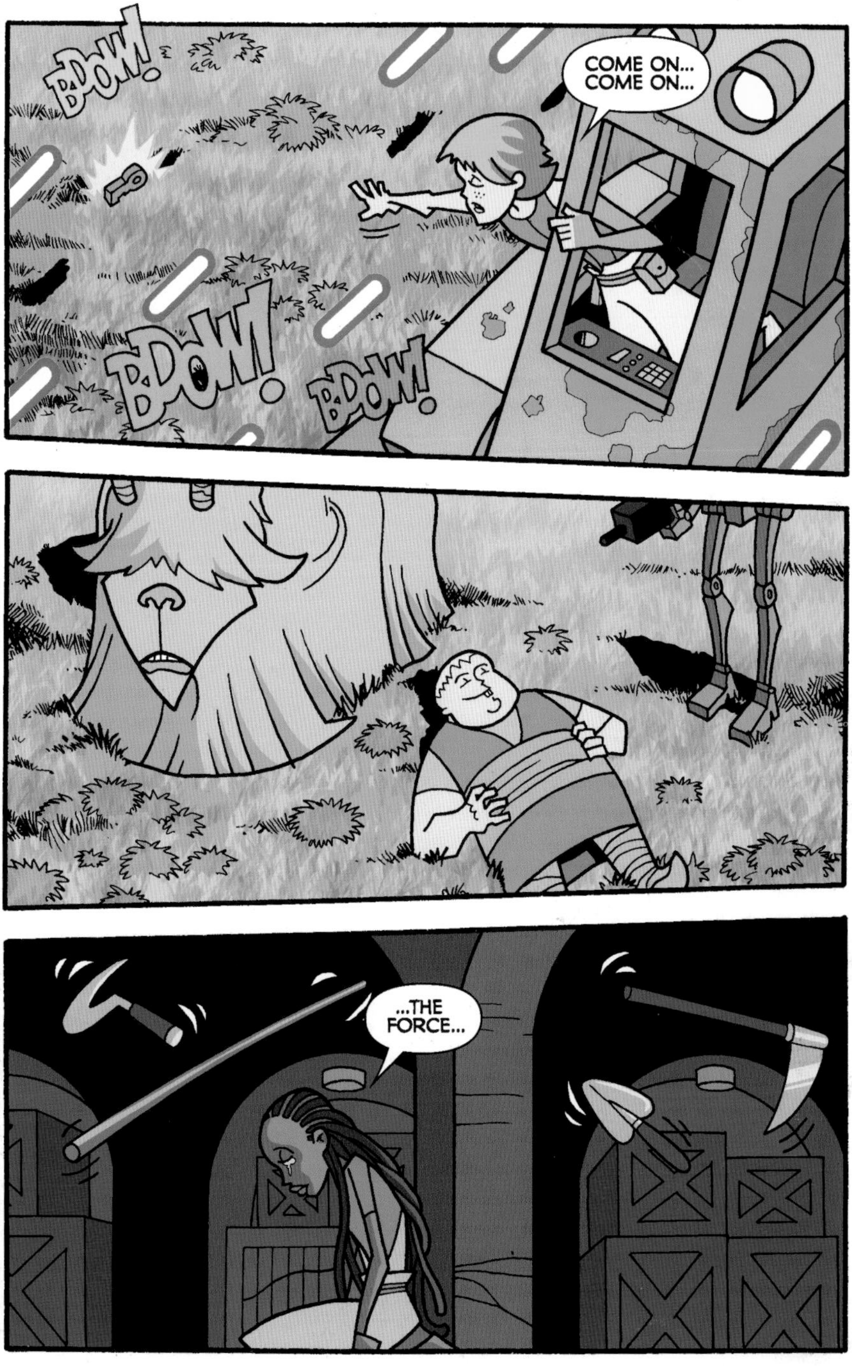
BDOW!
COME ON...
COME ON...
BDOW!
BDOW!
...THE
FORCE...

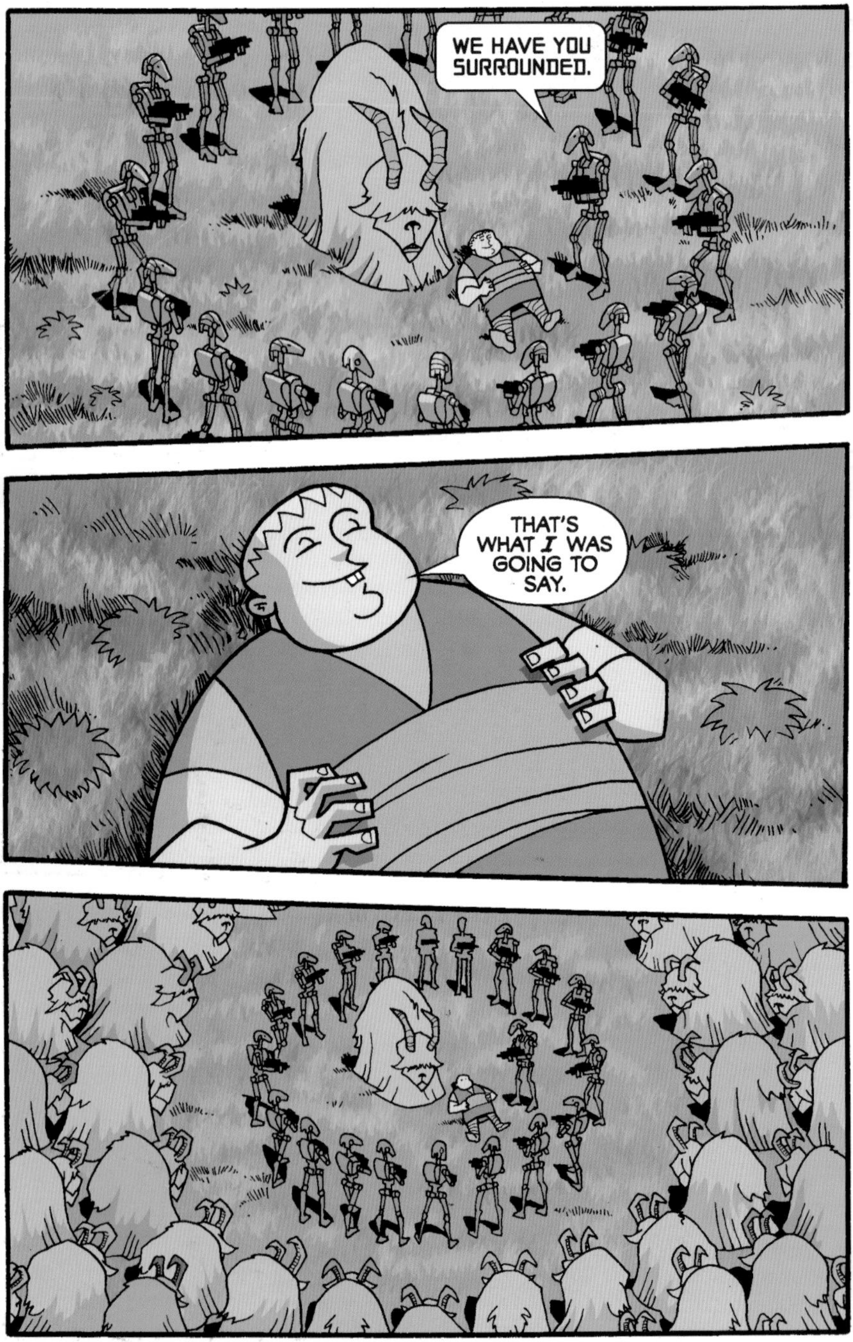
WE HAVE YOU SURROUNDED.
THAT'S WHAT *I* WAS GOING TO SAY.

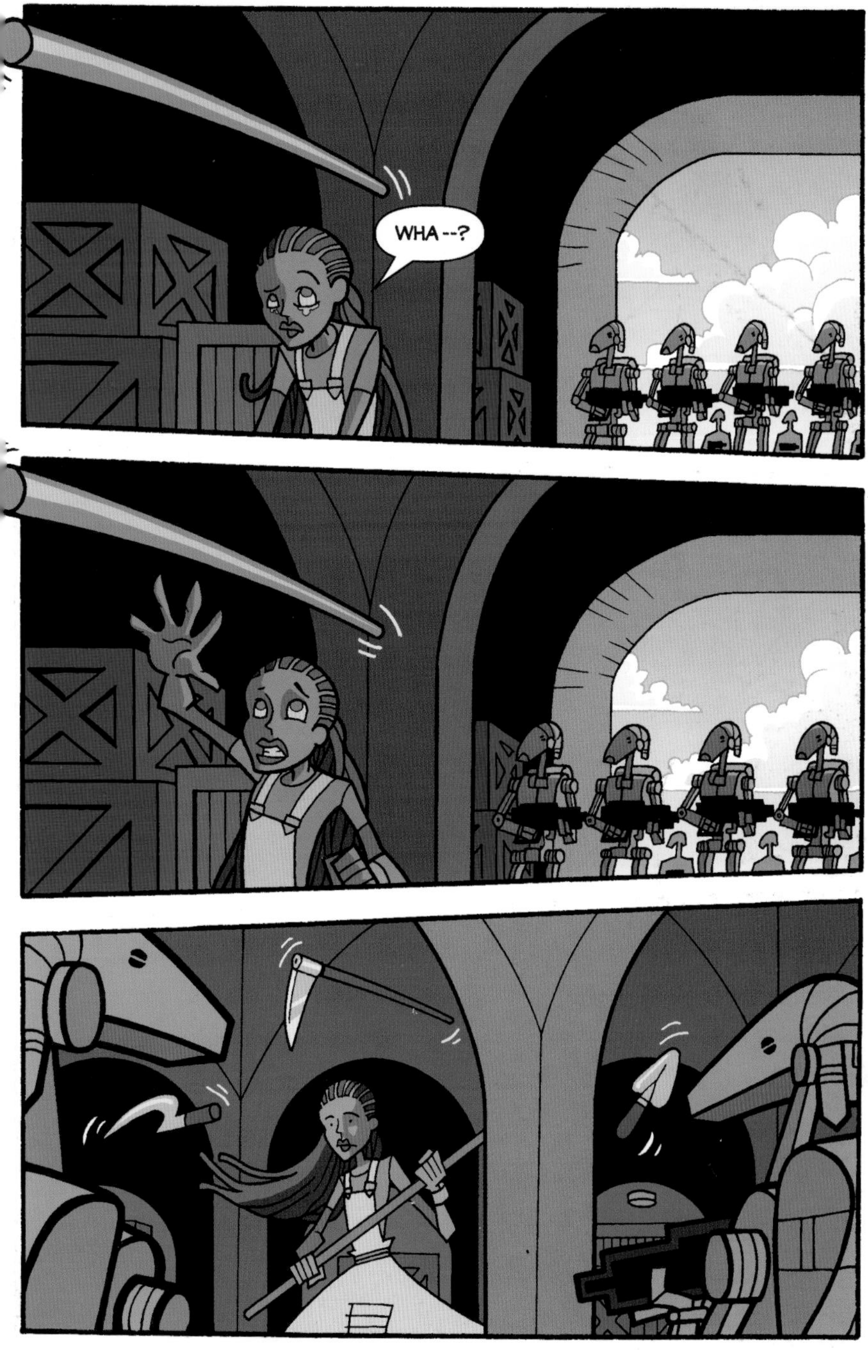
WHA--?

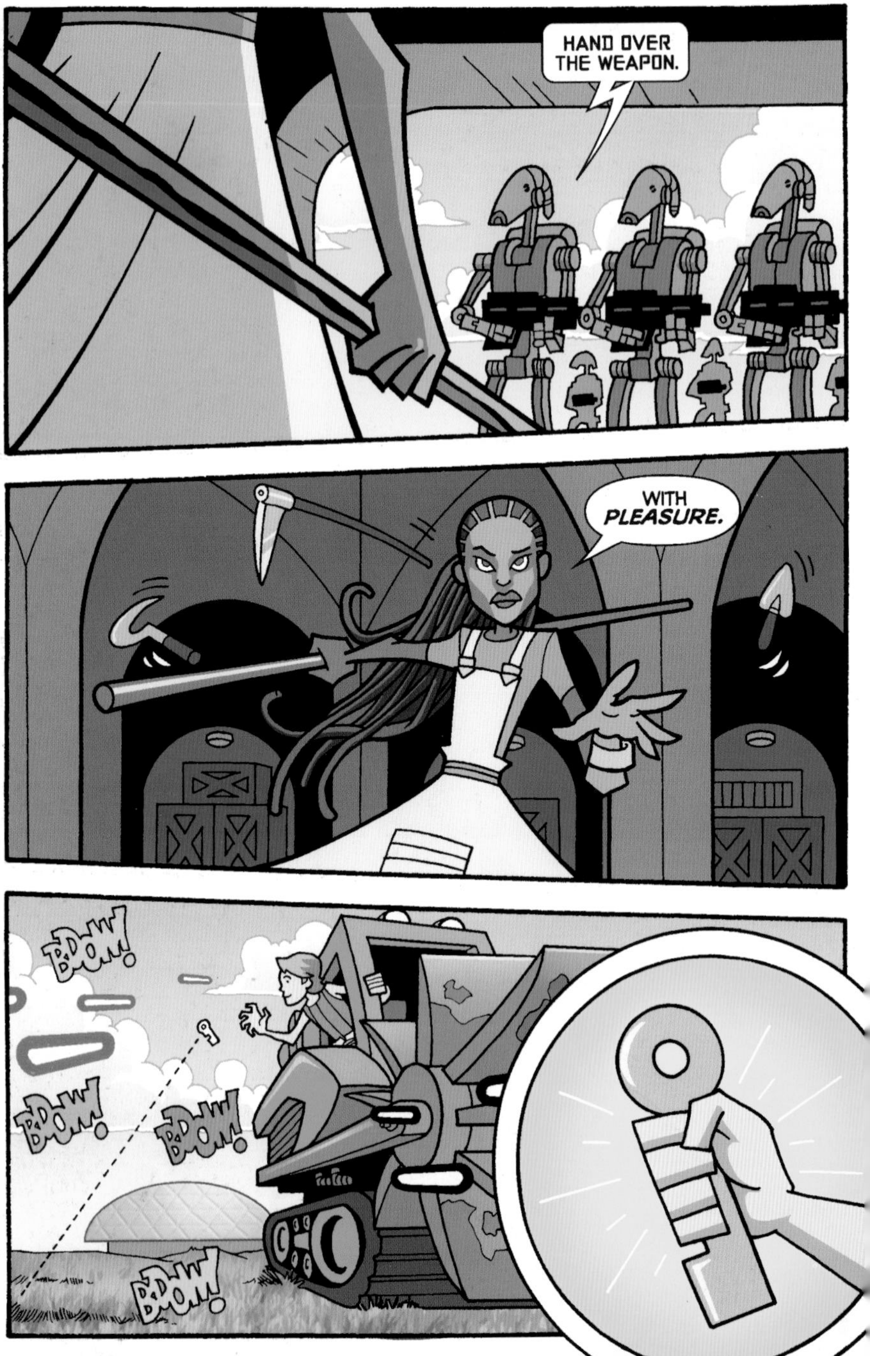
HAND OVER THE WEAPON.
WITH *PLEASURE.*
BADOOM!
BADOOM!
BADOOM!
BADOOM!

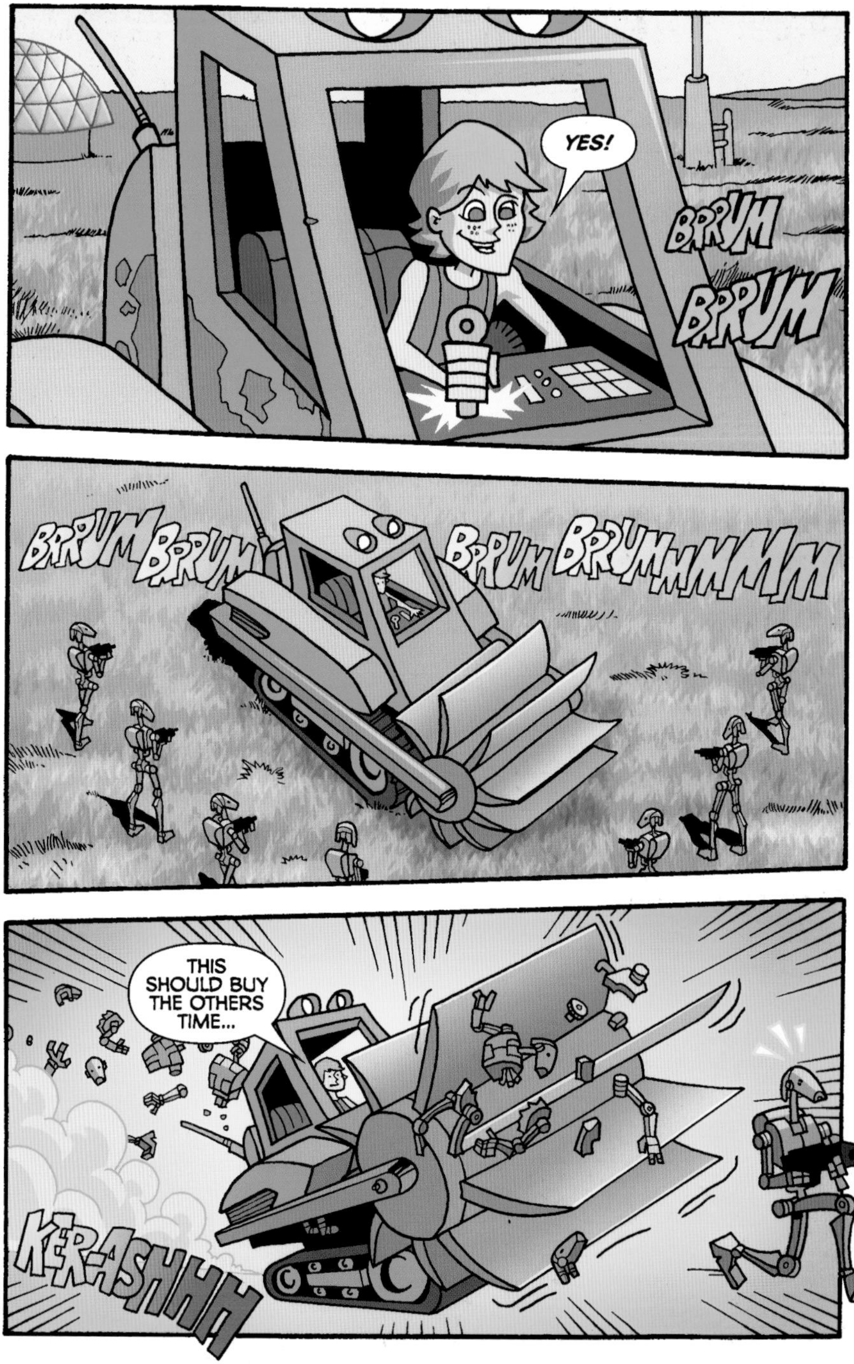
YES!
BRRUM
BRRUM
BRRUM BRRUM
BRRUM BRRUMMMMMM
THIS SHOULD BUY THE OTHERS TIME...
KER-ASHHH

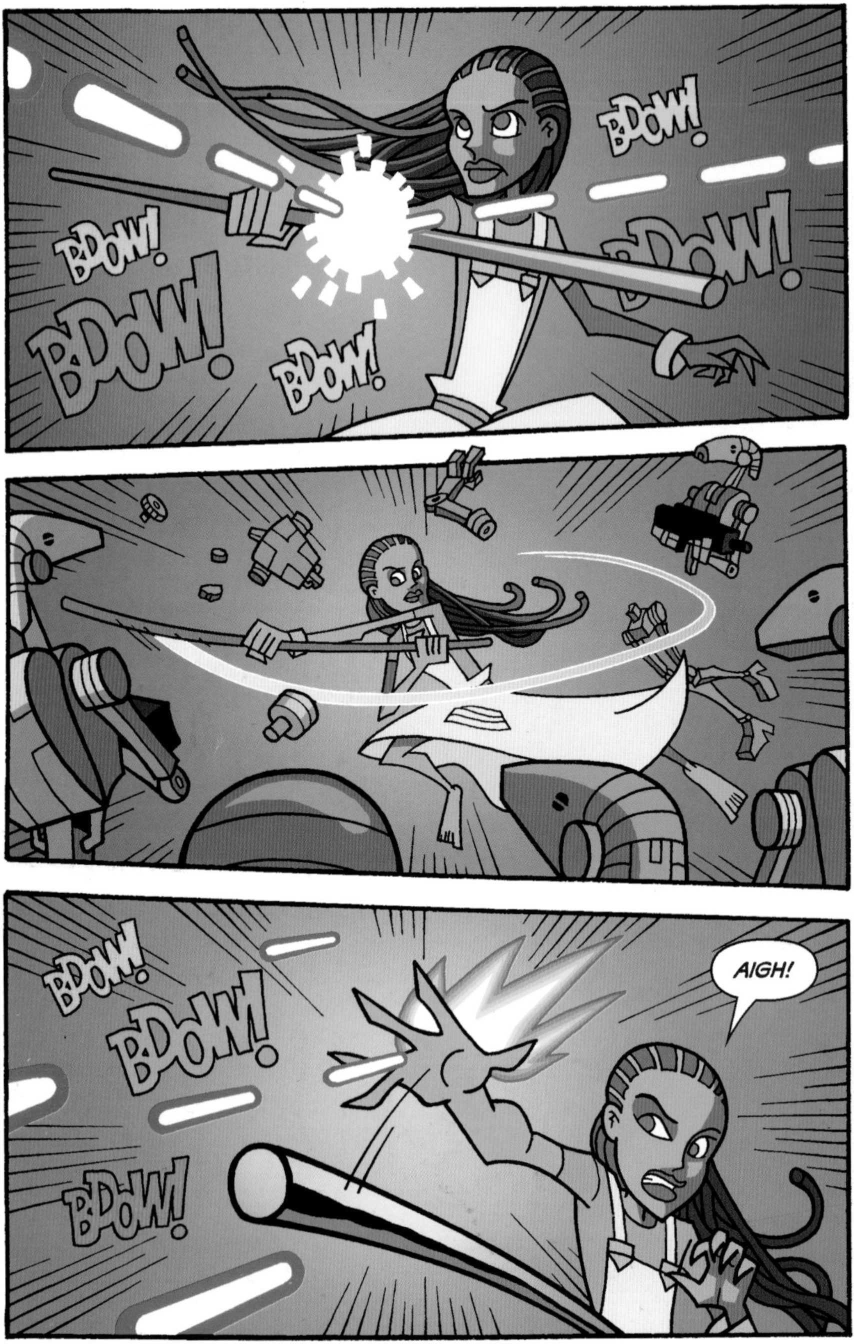
BDOW!
BDOW!
BDOW!
BDOW!
BDOW!
BDOW!
BDOW!
BDOW!
AIGH!

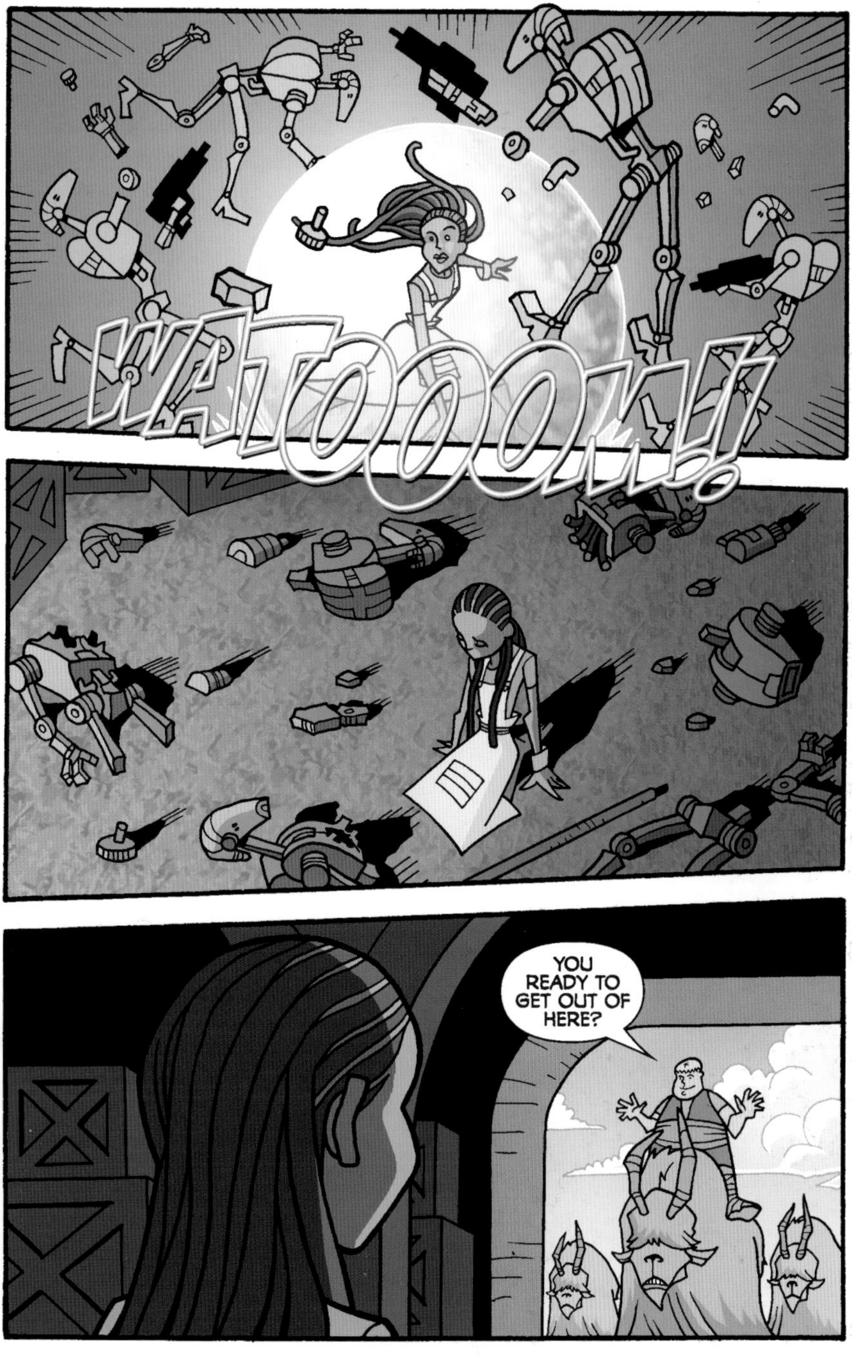
WATOOOM!!
YOU READY TO GET OUT OF HERE?

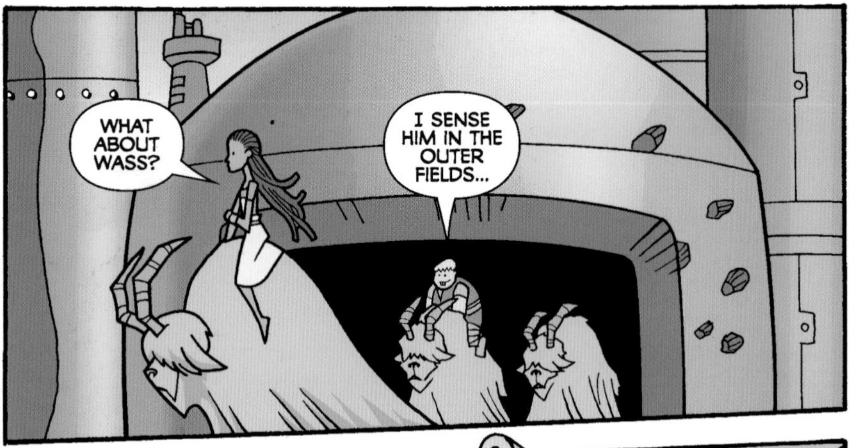
WHAT ABOUT WASS?
I SENSE HIM IN THE OUTER FIELDS...

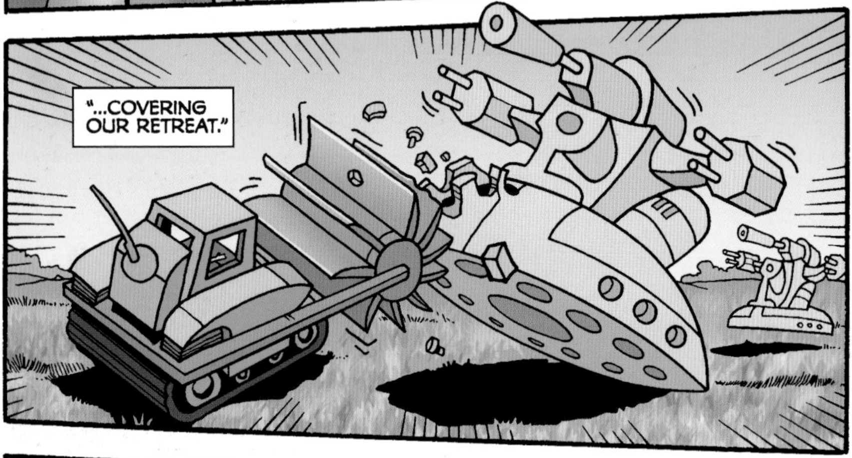
"...COVERING OUR RETREAT."

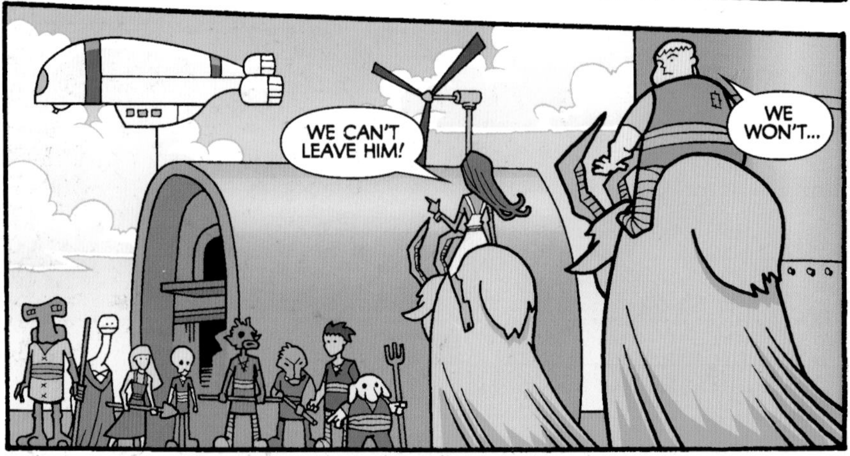
WE CAN'T LEAVE HIM!
WE WON'T...

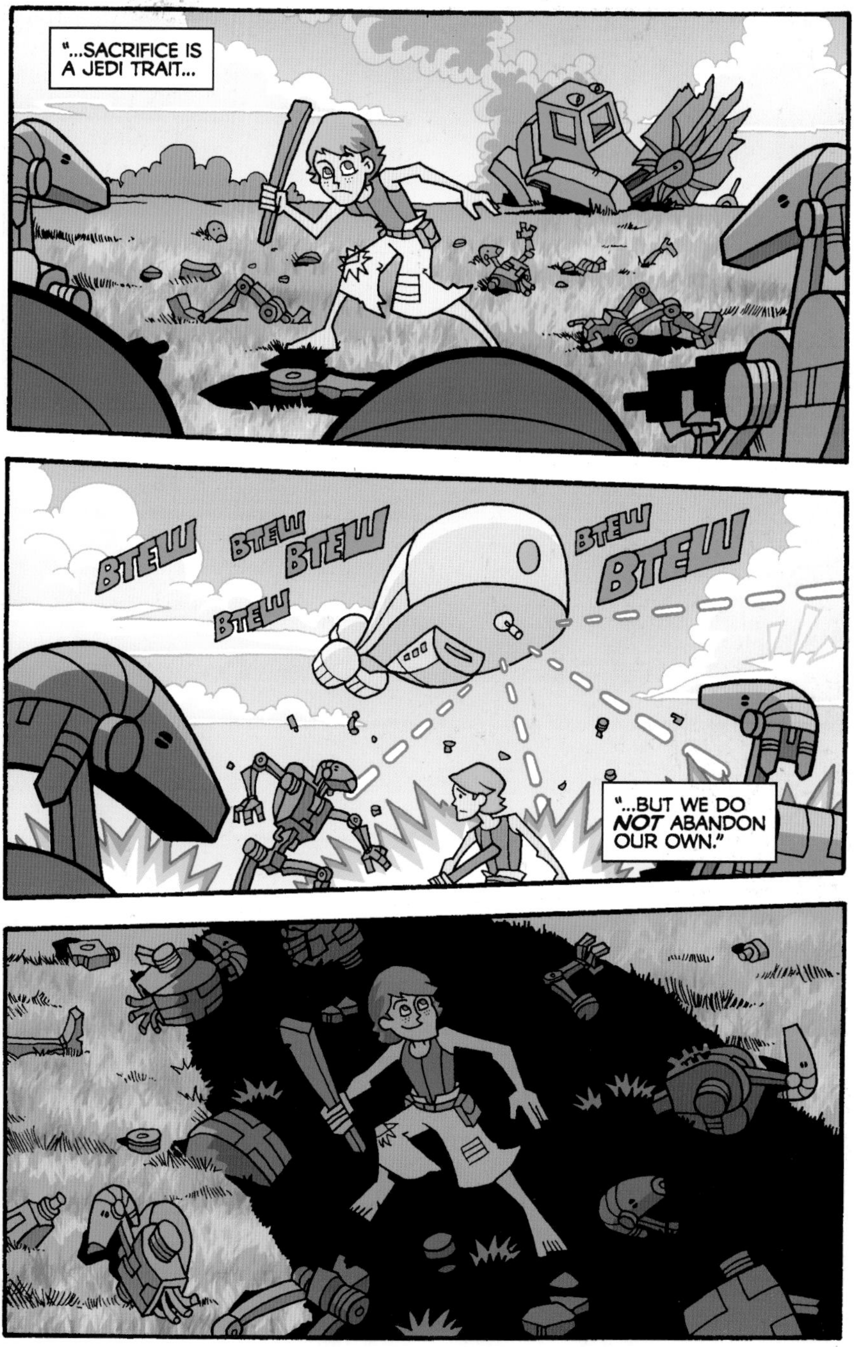
"...SACRIFICE IS A JEDI TRAIT...
BTEW
BTEW
BTEW
BTEW
BTEW
BTEW
"...BUT WE DO NOT ABANDON OUR OWN."

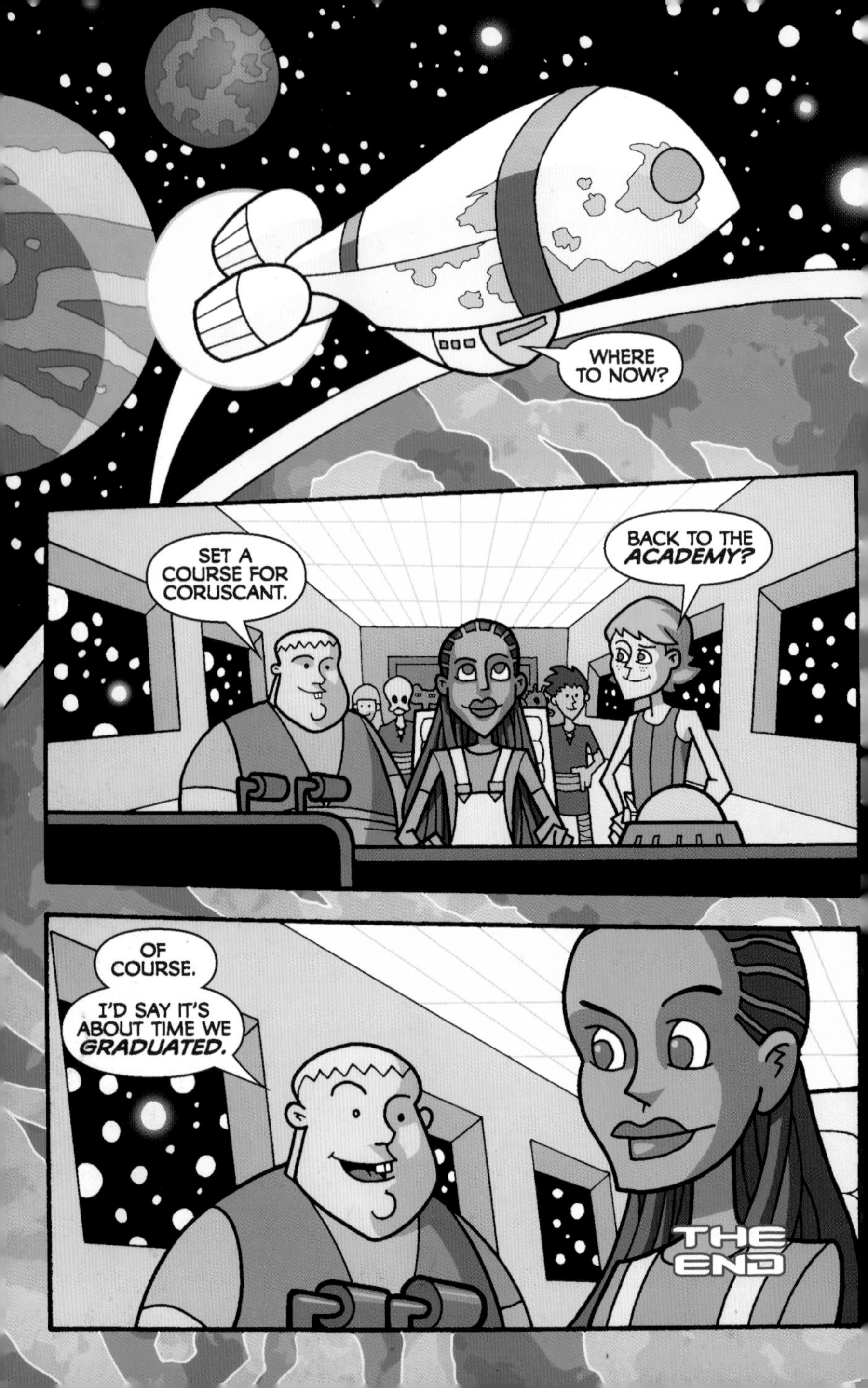
WHERE TO NOW?
SET A COURSE FOR CORUSCANT.
BACK TO THE *ACADEMY?*
OF COURSE.
I'D SAY IT'S ABOUT TIME WE *GRADUATED.*
THE END

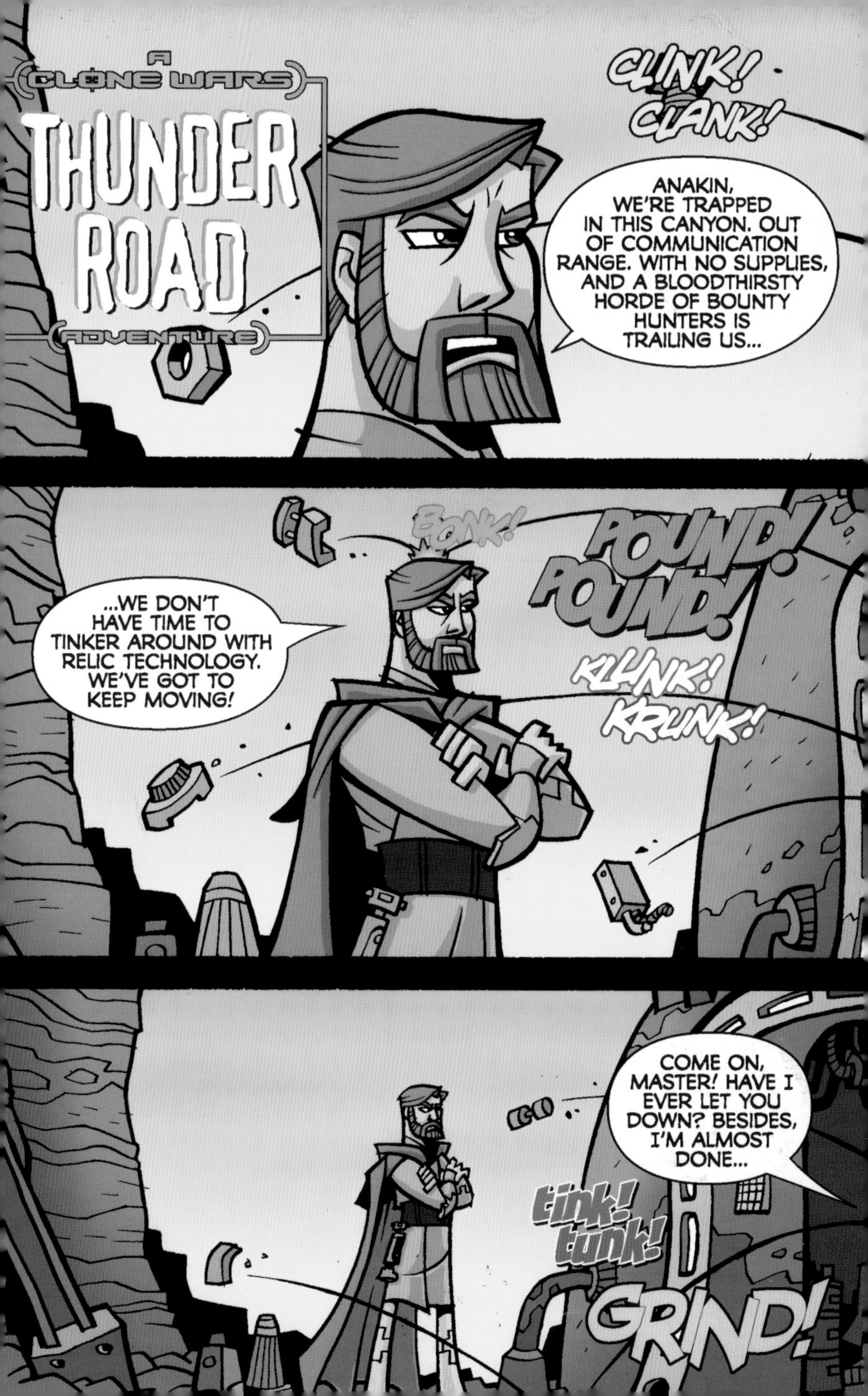
A CLONE WARS
THUNDER ROAD
ADVENTURE
CLINK! CLANK!
ANAKIN, WE'RE TRAPPED IN THIS CANYON. OUT OF COMMUNICATION RANGE. WITH NO SUPPLIES, AND A BLOODTHIRSTY HORDE OF BOUNTY HUNTERS IS TRAILING US...
BONK!
POUND! POUND!
...WE DON'T HAVE TIME TO TINKER AROUND WITH RELIC TECHNOLOGY. WE'VE GOT TO KEEP MOVING!
KLUNK! KRUNK!
COME ON, MASTER! HAVE I EVER LET YOU DOWN? BESIDES, I'M ALMOST DONE...
tink! tunk!
GRIND!

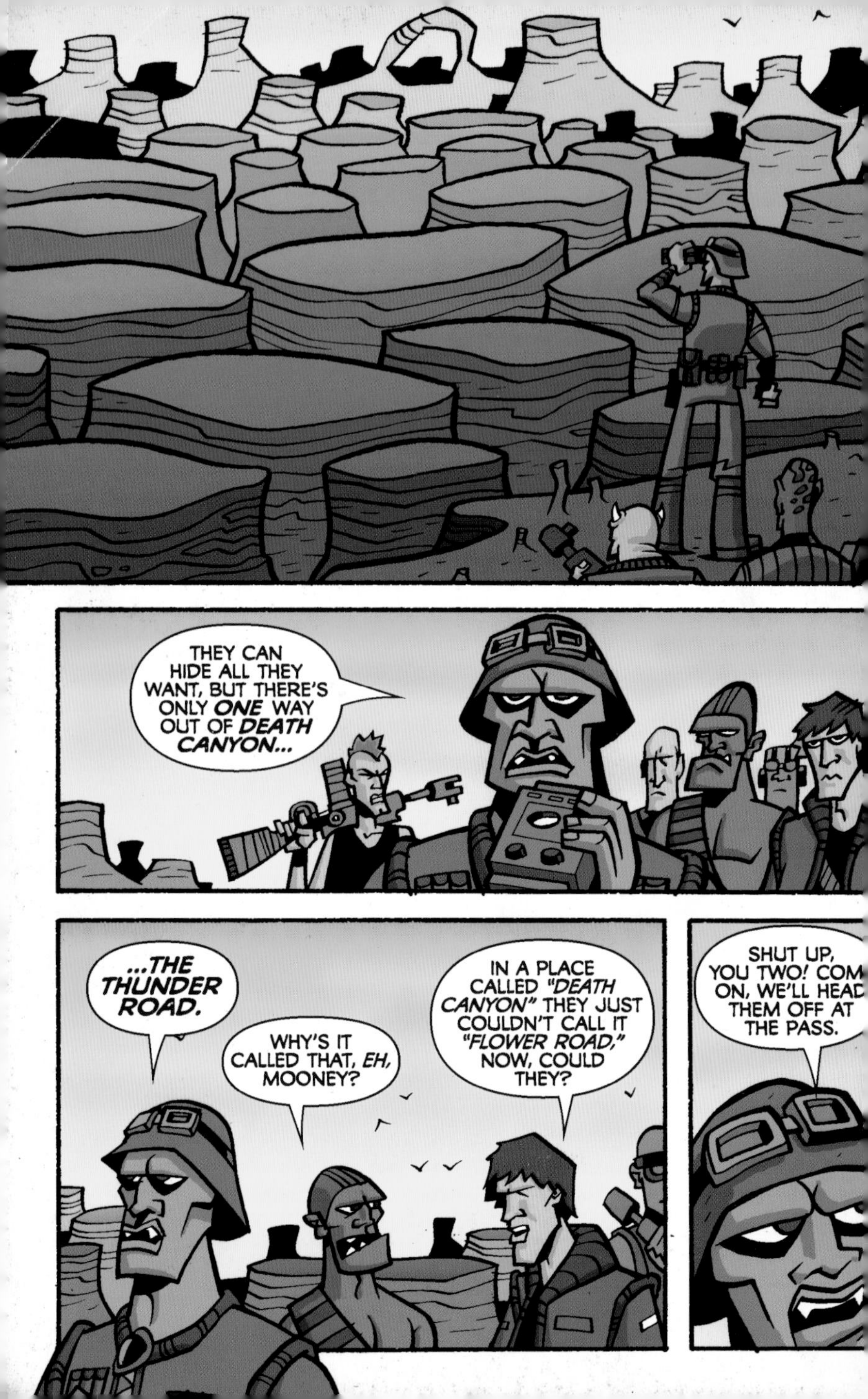
THEY CAN HIDE ALL THEY WANT, BUT THERE'S ONLY *ONE* WAY OUT OF *DEATH CANYON...*
...THE THUNDER ROAD.
WHY'S IT CALLED THAT, *EH,* MOONEY?
IN A PLACE CALLED *"DEATH CANYON"* THEY JUST COULDN'T CALL IT *"FLOWER ROAD,"* NOW, COULD THEY?
SHUT UP, YOU TWO! COM ON, WE'LL HEAD THEM OFF AT THE PASS.

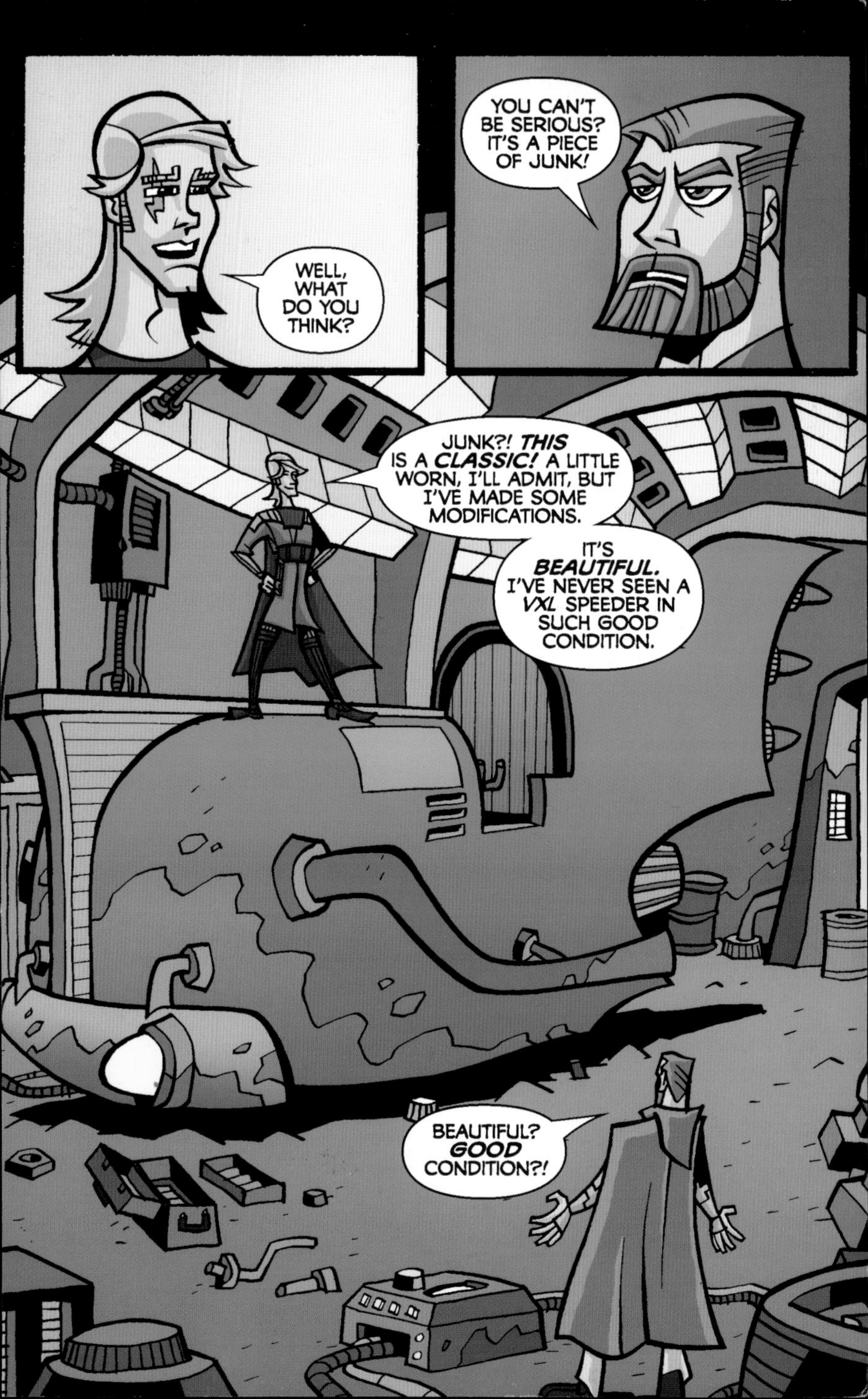
WELL, WHAT DO YOU THINK?
YOU CAN'T BE SERIOUS? IT'S A PIECE OF JUNK!
JUNK?! *THIS* IS A *CLASSIC!* A LITTLE WORN, I'LL ADMIT, BUT I'VE MADE SOME MODIFICATIONS.
IT'S *BEAUTIFUL.* I'VE NEVER SEEN A *VXL* SPEEDER IN SUCH GOOD CONDITION.
BEAUTIFUL? *GOOD* CONDITION?!

CLASSIC OR NOT, I DON'T THINK IT'LL GO TEN METERS BEFORE FALLING APART.

YOU'D BETTER HOLD ON, MASTER. THIS IS GONNA BE A *FAST* RIDE!

HUMPF...I SERIOUSLY DOUBT --

--THAAAAAAT!!

VWOOSH!!

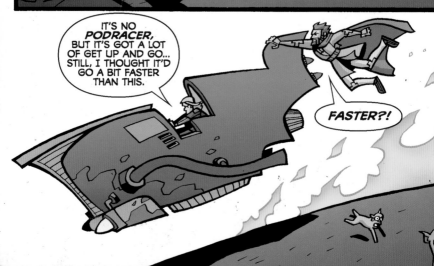

IT'S NO *PODRACER,* BUT IT'S GOT A LOT OF GET UP AND GO... STILL, I THOUGHT IT'D GO A BIT FASTER THAN THIS.

FASTER?!

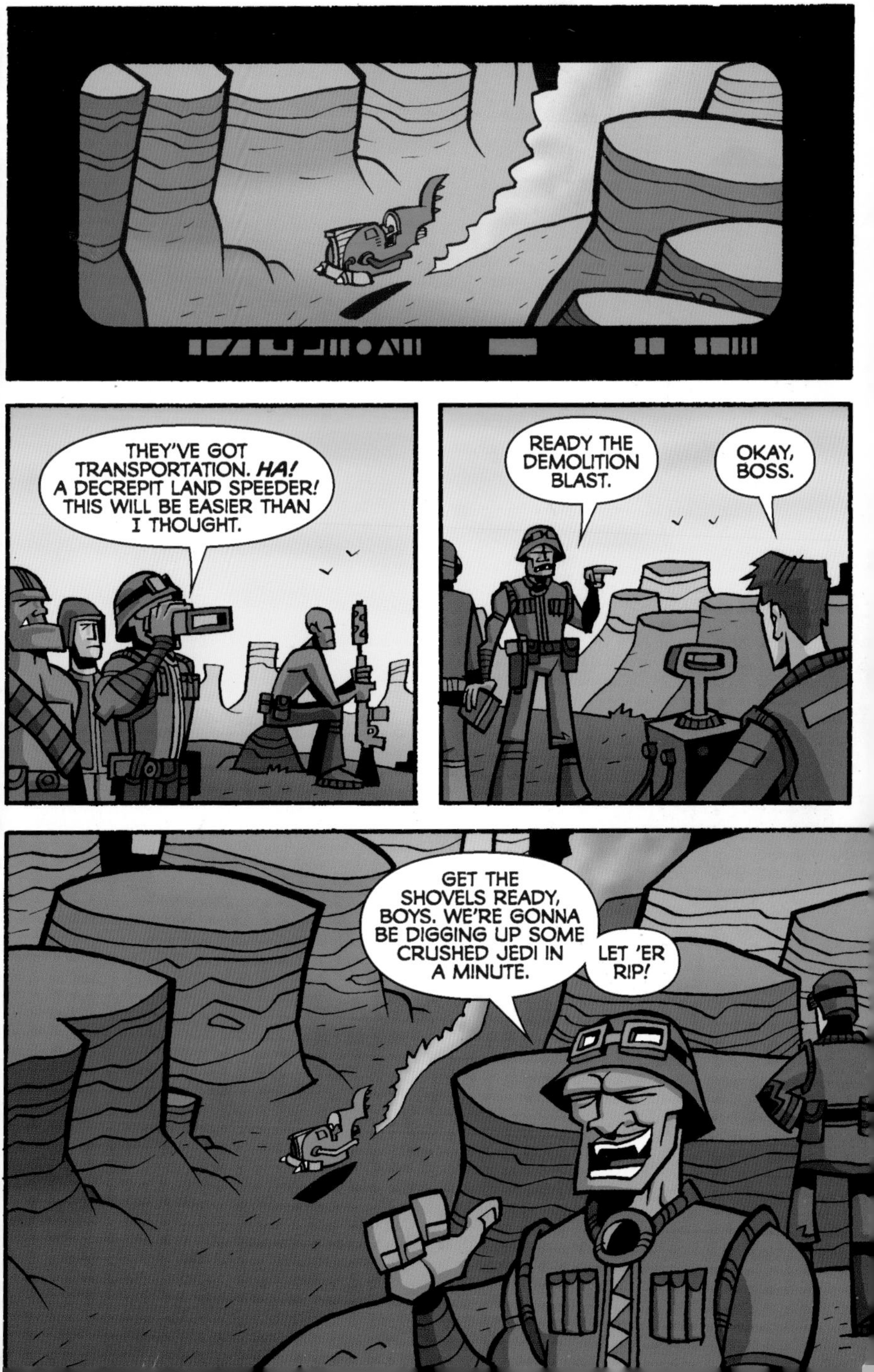
THEY'VE GOT TRANSPORTATION. ***HA!*** A DECREPIT LAND SPEEDER! THIS WILL BE EASIER THAN I THOUGHT.
READY THE DEMOLITION BLAST.
OKAY, BOSS.
GET THE SHOVELS READY, BOYS. WE'RE GONNA BE DIGGING UP SOME CRUSHED JEDI IN A MINUTE.
LET 'ER RIP!

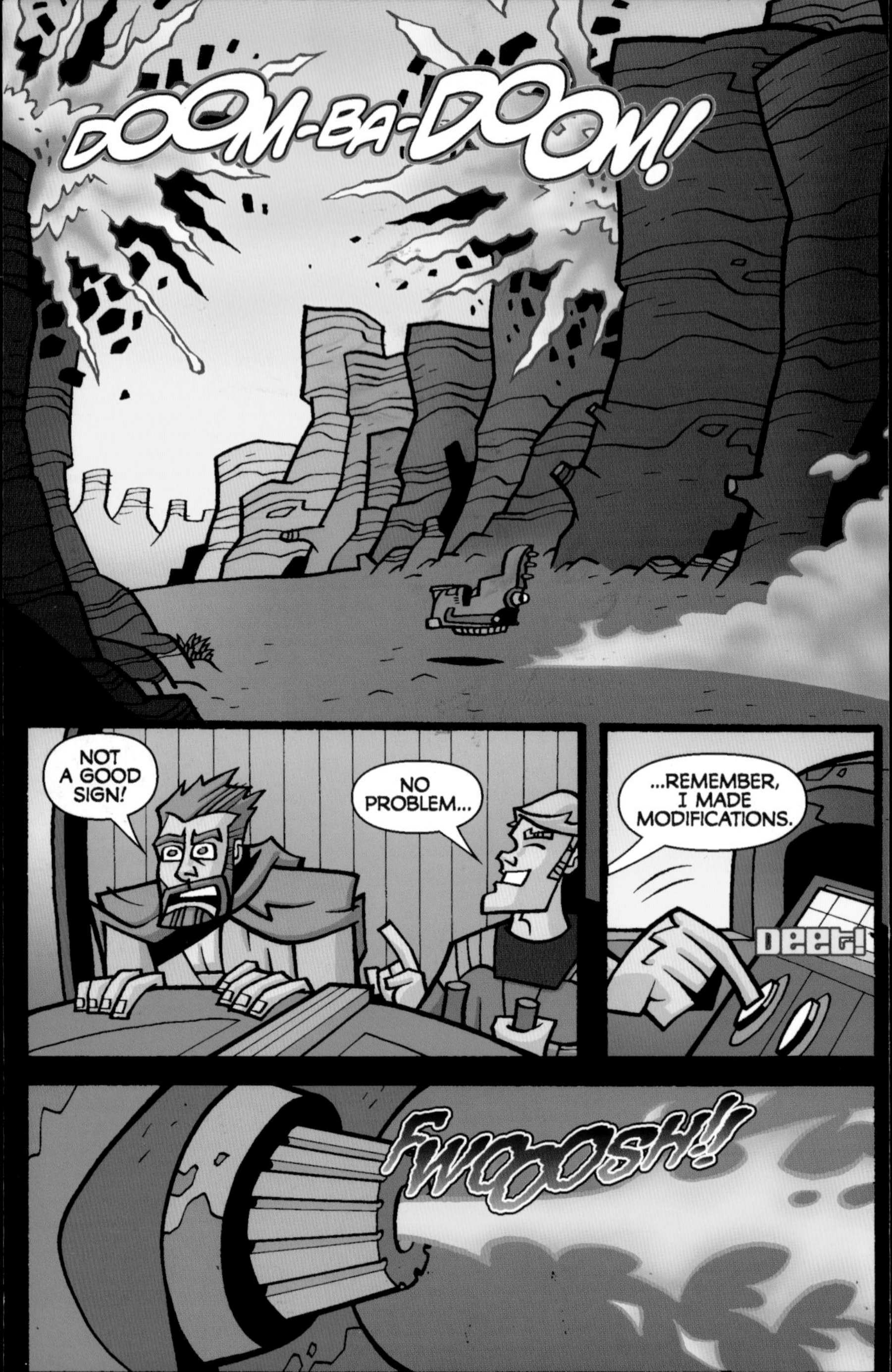
DOOM-BA-DOOOM!
NOT A GOOD SIGN!
NO PROBLEM...
...REMEMBER, I MADE MODIFICATIONS.
DEET!
FWOOOSH!!

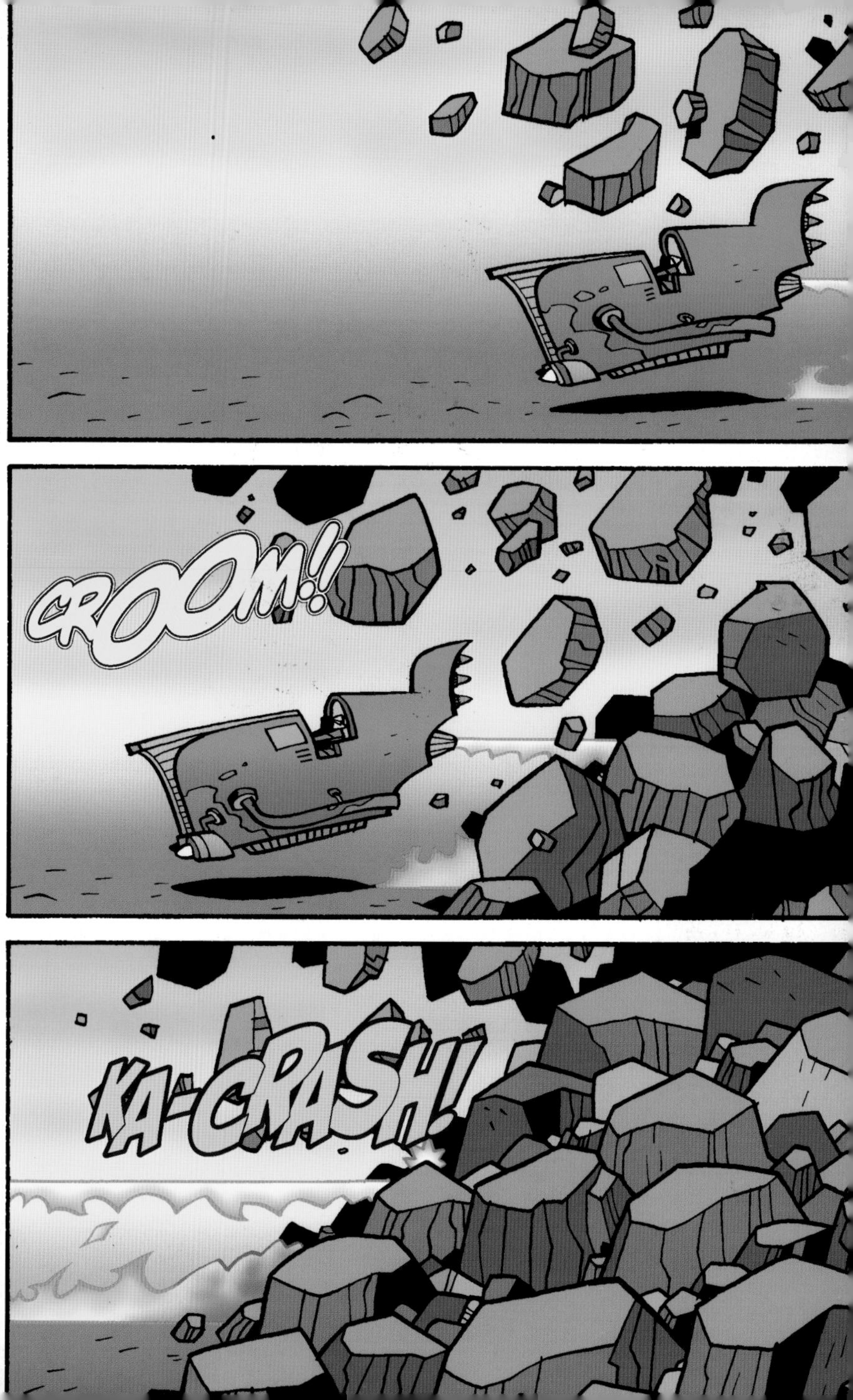
CROOM!!
KA-CRASH!

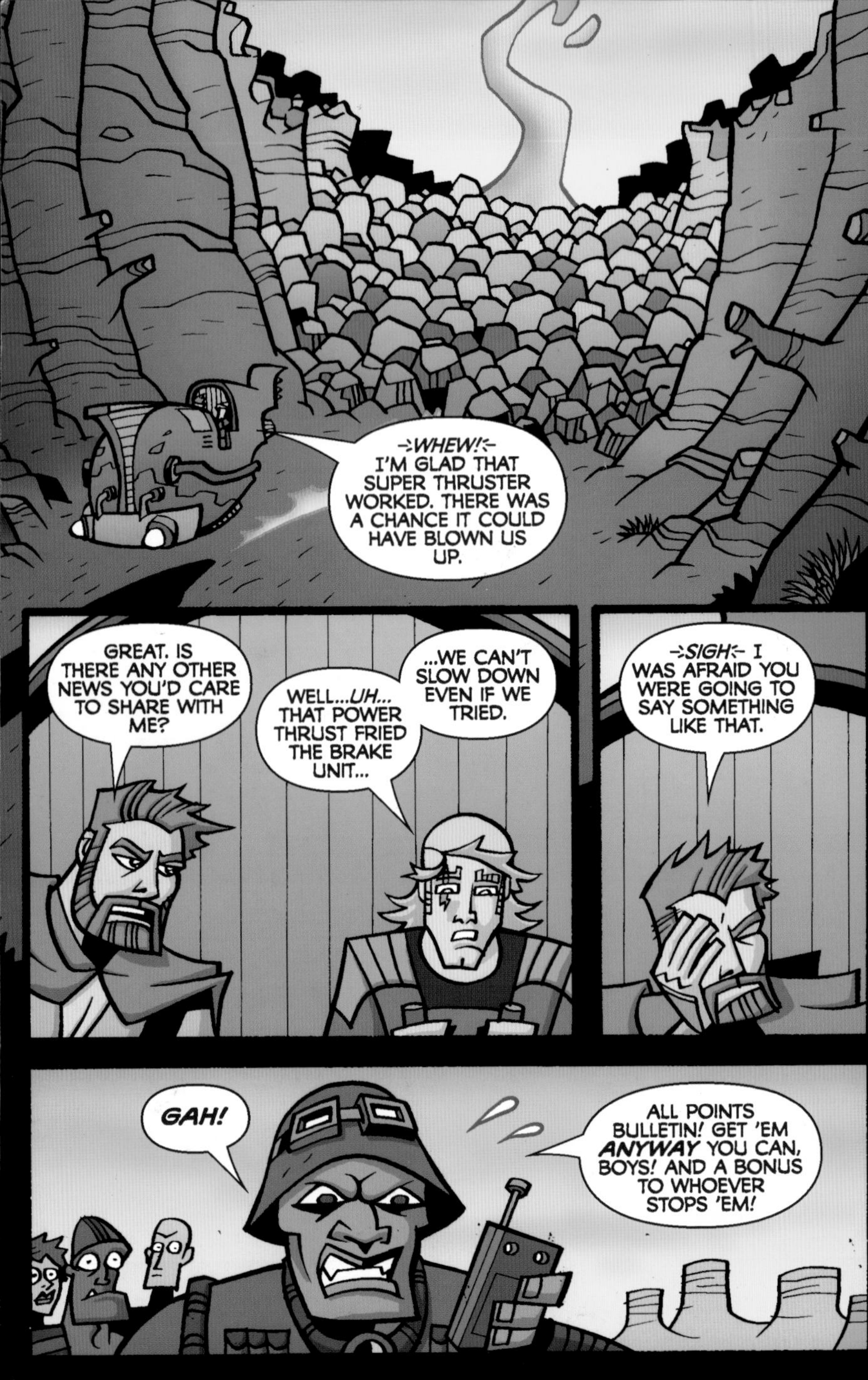
-WHEW!- I'M GLAD THAT SUPER THRUSTER WORKED. THERE WAS A CHANCE IT COULD HAVE BLOWN US UP.
GREAT. IS THERE ANY OTHER NEWS YOU'D CARE TO SHARE WITH ME?
WELL...UH... THAT POWER THRUST FRIED THE BRAKE UNIT...
...WE CAN'T SLOW DOWN EVEN IF WE TRIED.
-SIGH- I WAS AFRAID YOU WERE GOING TO SAY SOMETHING LIKE THAT.
GAH!
ALL POINTS BULLETIN! GET 'EM ANYWAY YOU CAN, BOYS! AND A BONUS TO WHOEVER STOPS 'EM!

FIRE WHEN READY!!
PLOOM!
TUNK!

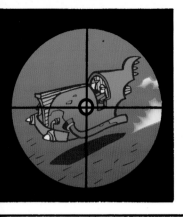

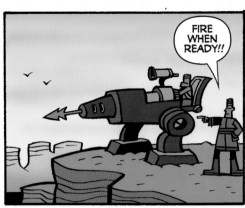

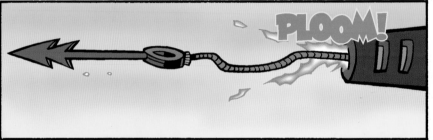

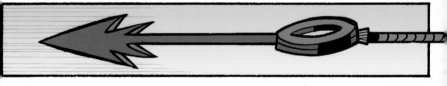

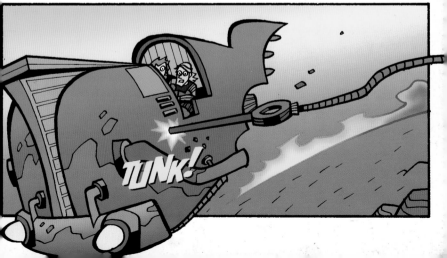

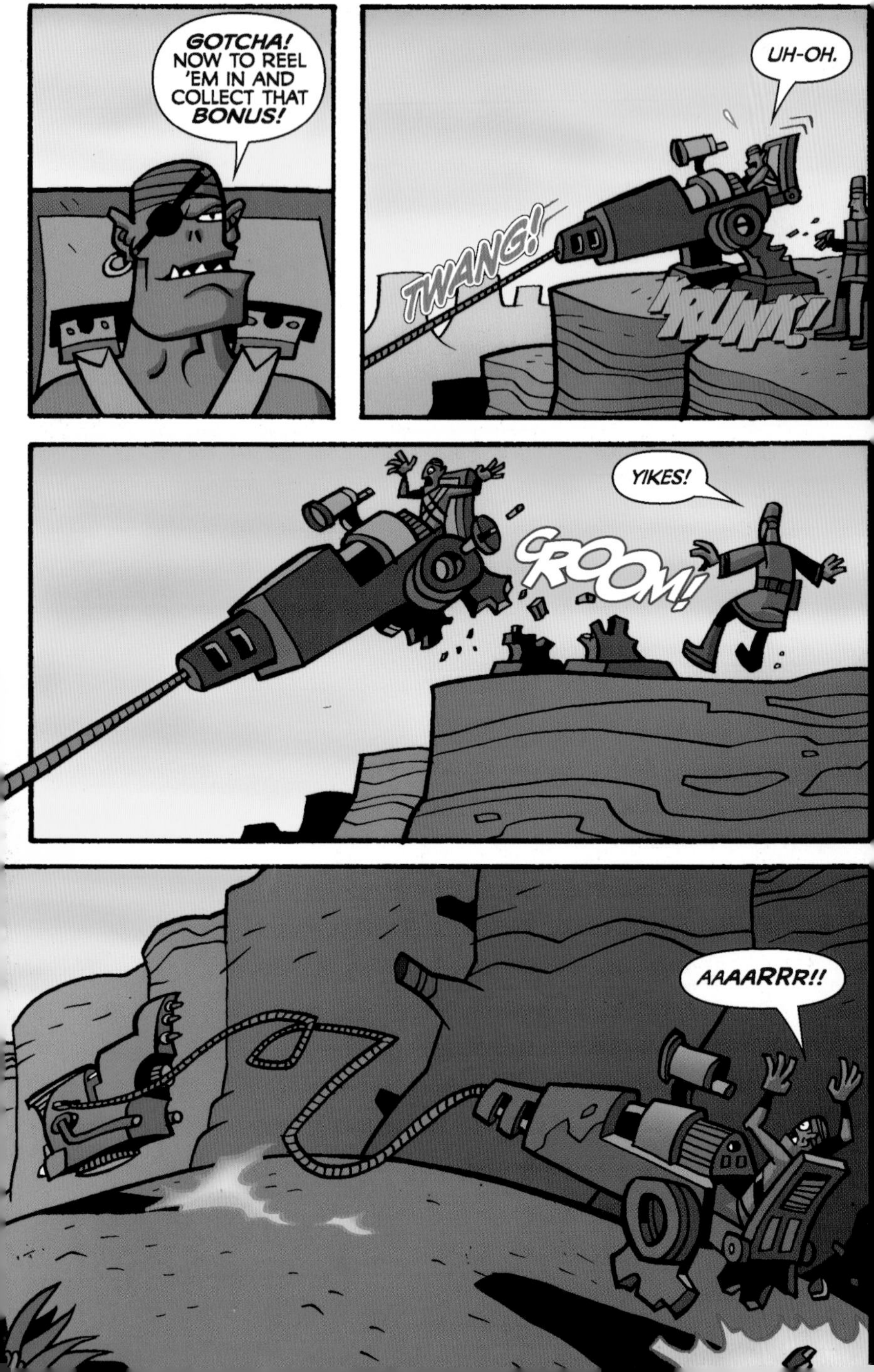
GOTCHA! NOW TO REEL 'EM IN AND COLLECT THAT BONUS!
UH-OH.
TWANG!
KRUNK!
YIKES!
CROOM!
AAAARRR!!

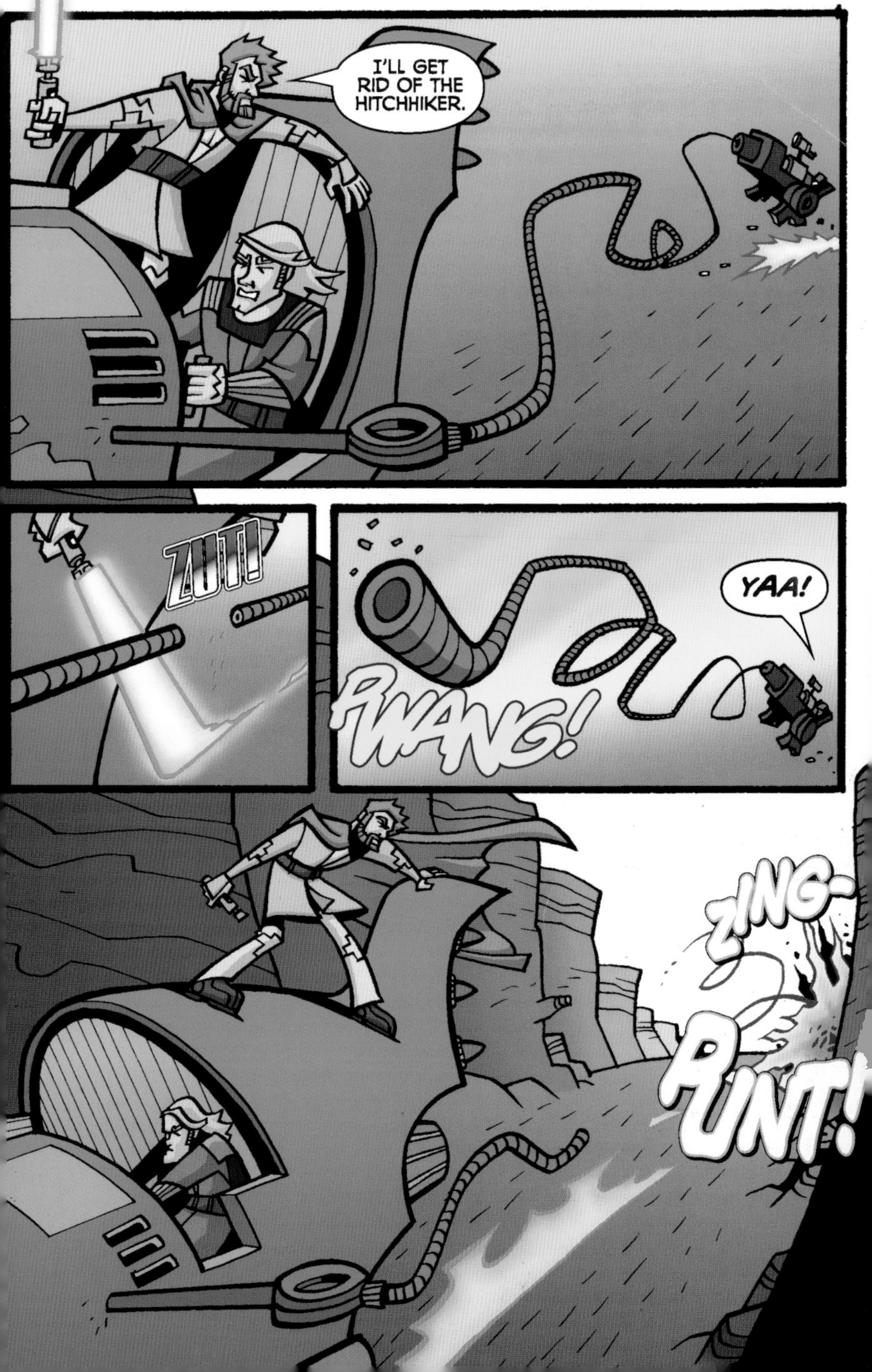
I'LL GET RID OF THE HITCHHIKER.
ZUT!
YAA!
PWANG!
ZING-
PUNT!

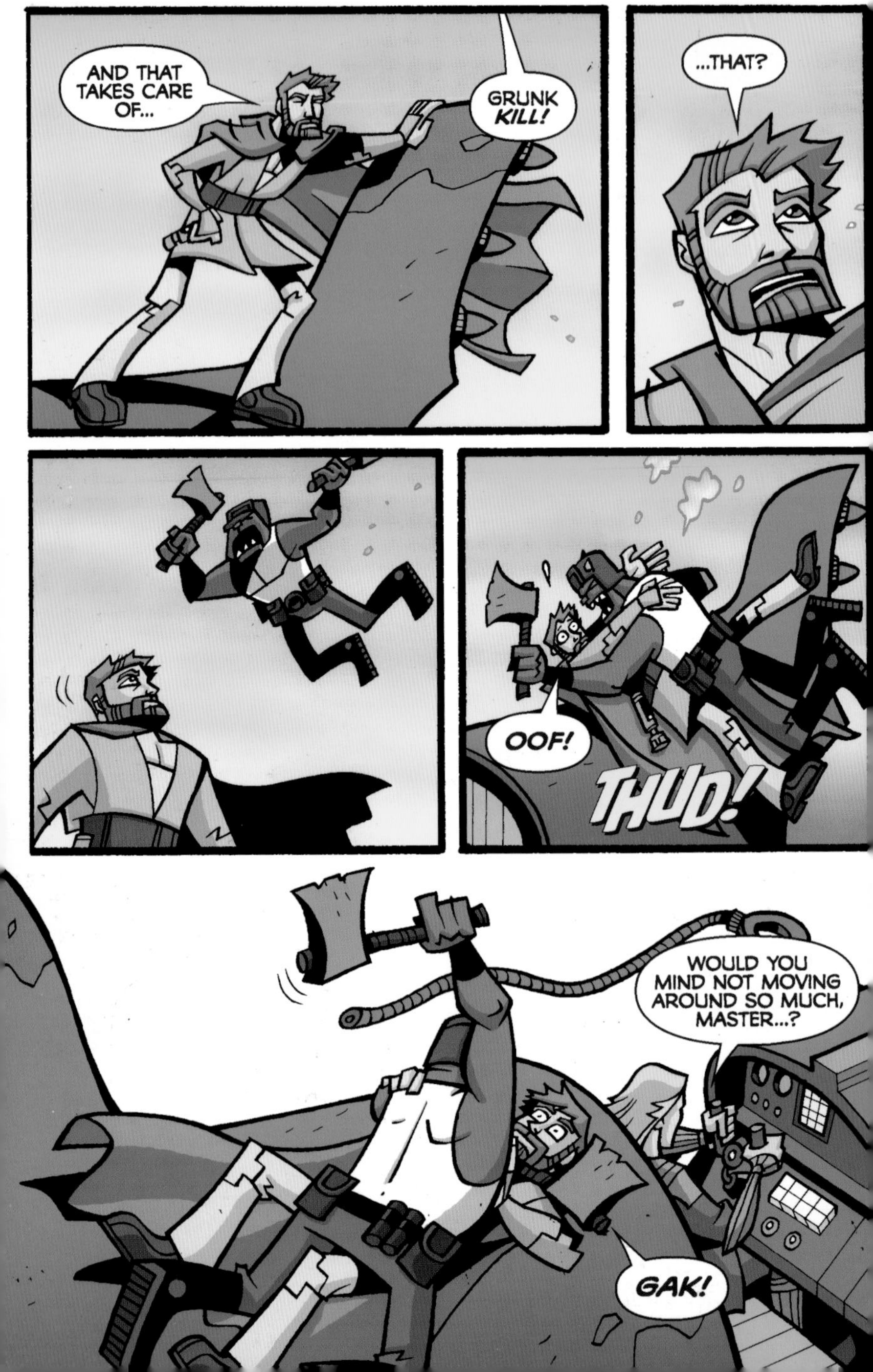
AND THAT TAKES CARE OF...
GRUNK KILL!
...THAT?
OOF!
THUD!
WOULD YOU MIND NOT MOVING AROUND SO MUCH, MASTER...?
GAK!

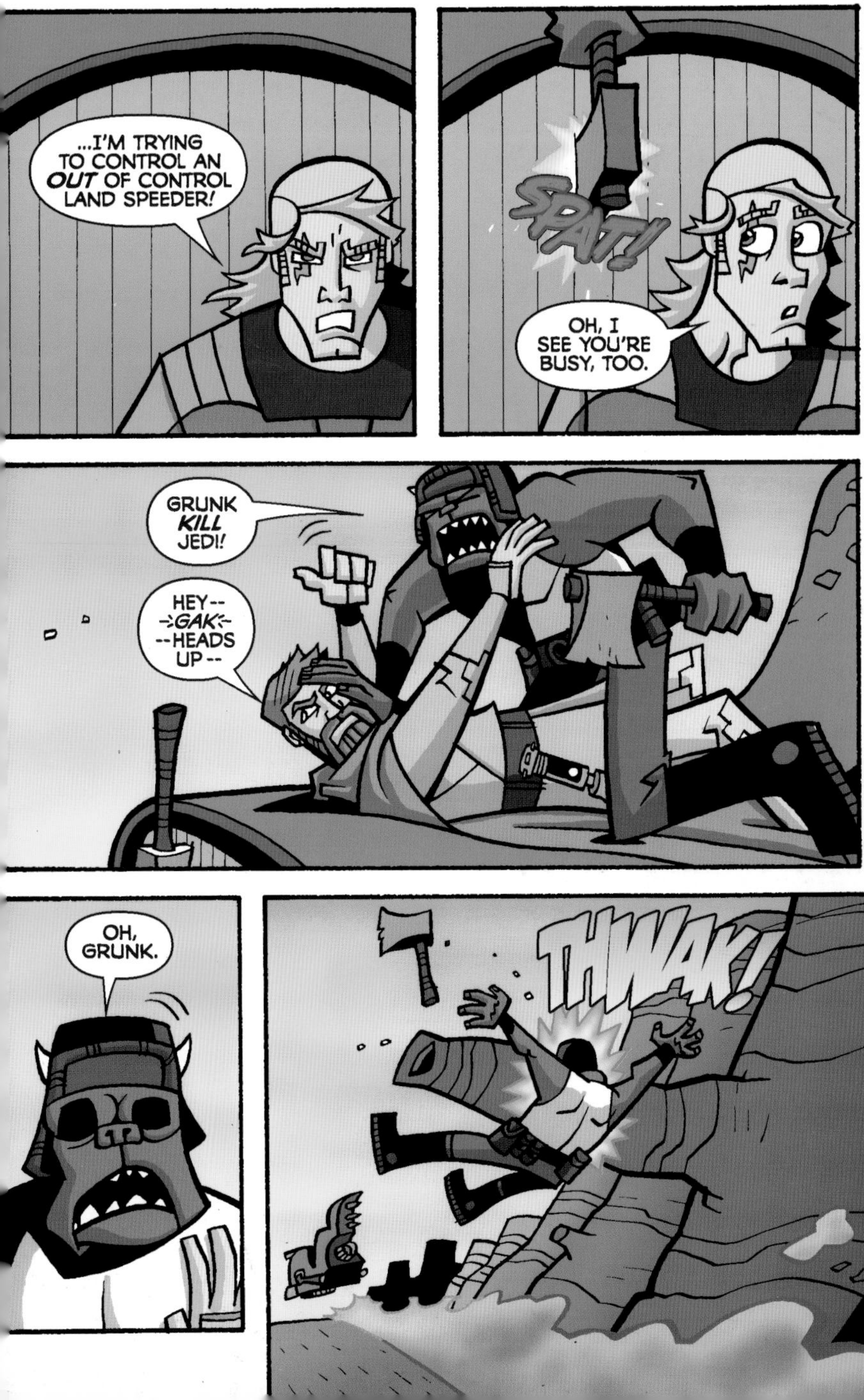
...I'M TRYING TO CONTROL AN OUT OF CONTROL LAND SPEEDER!
SPAT!
OH, I SEE YOU'RE BUSY, TOO.
GRUNK KILL JEDI!
HEY-- GAK --HEADS UP--
OH, GRUNK.
THWAK!

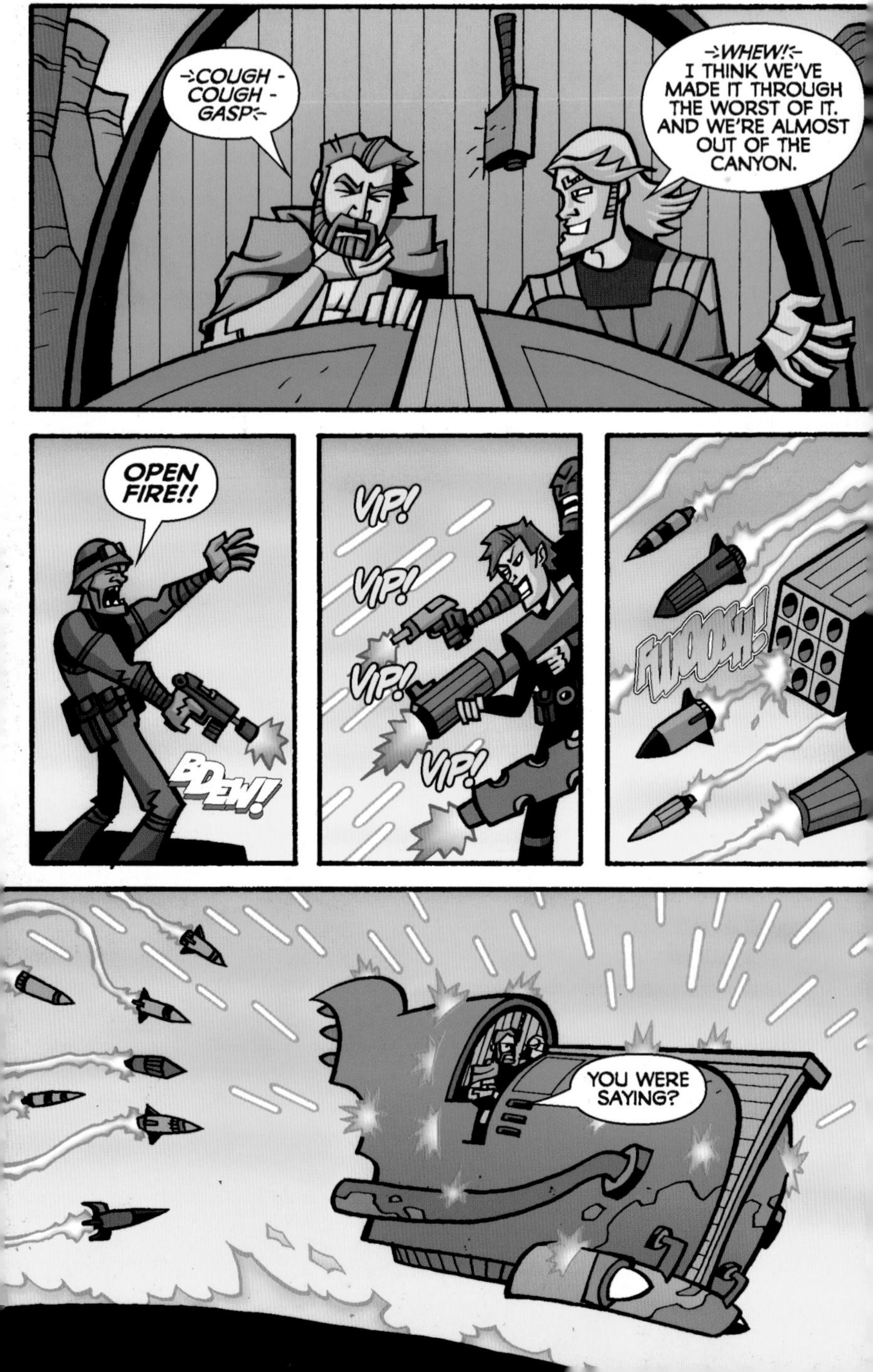
-COUGH - COUGH - GASP-
-WHEW!- I THINK WE'VE MADE IT THROUGH THE WORST OF IT. AND WE'RE ALMOST OUT OF THE CANYON.
OPEN FIRE!!
BDEW!
VIP!
VIP!
VIP!
VIP!
FWOOSH!
YOU WERE SAYING?

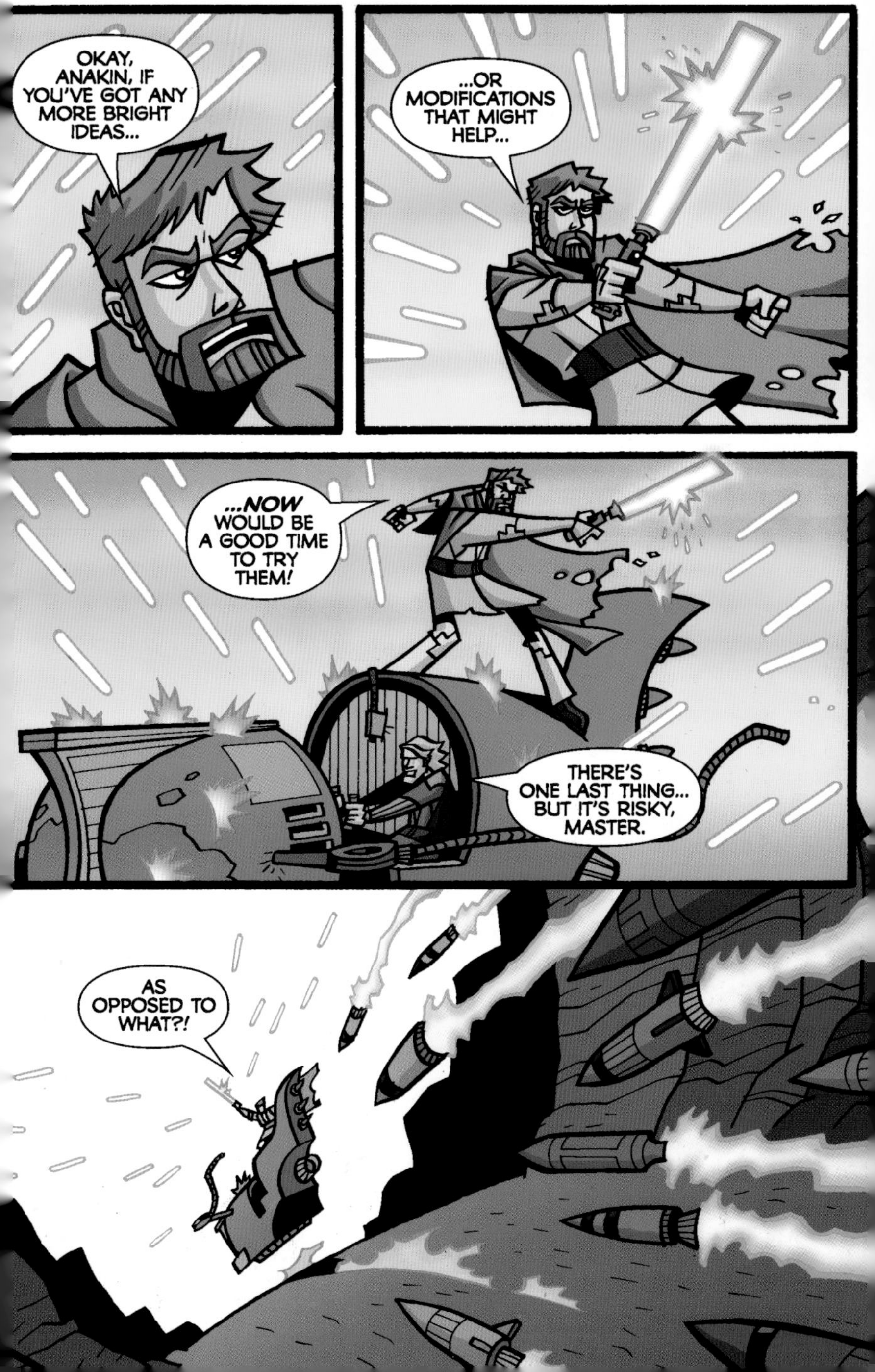

OKAY, ANAKIN, IF YOU'VE GOT ANY MORE BRIGHT IDEAS...
...OR MODIFICATIONS THAT MIGHT HELP...
...*NOW* WOULD BE A GOOD TIME TO TRY THEM!
THERE'S ONE LAST THING... BUT IT'S RISKY, MASTER.
AS OPPOSED TO WHAT?!

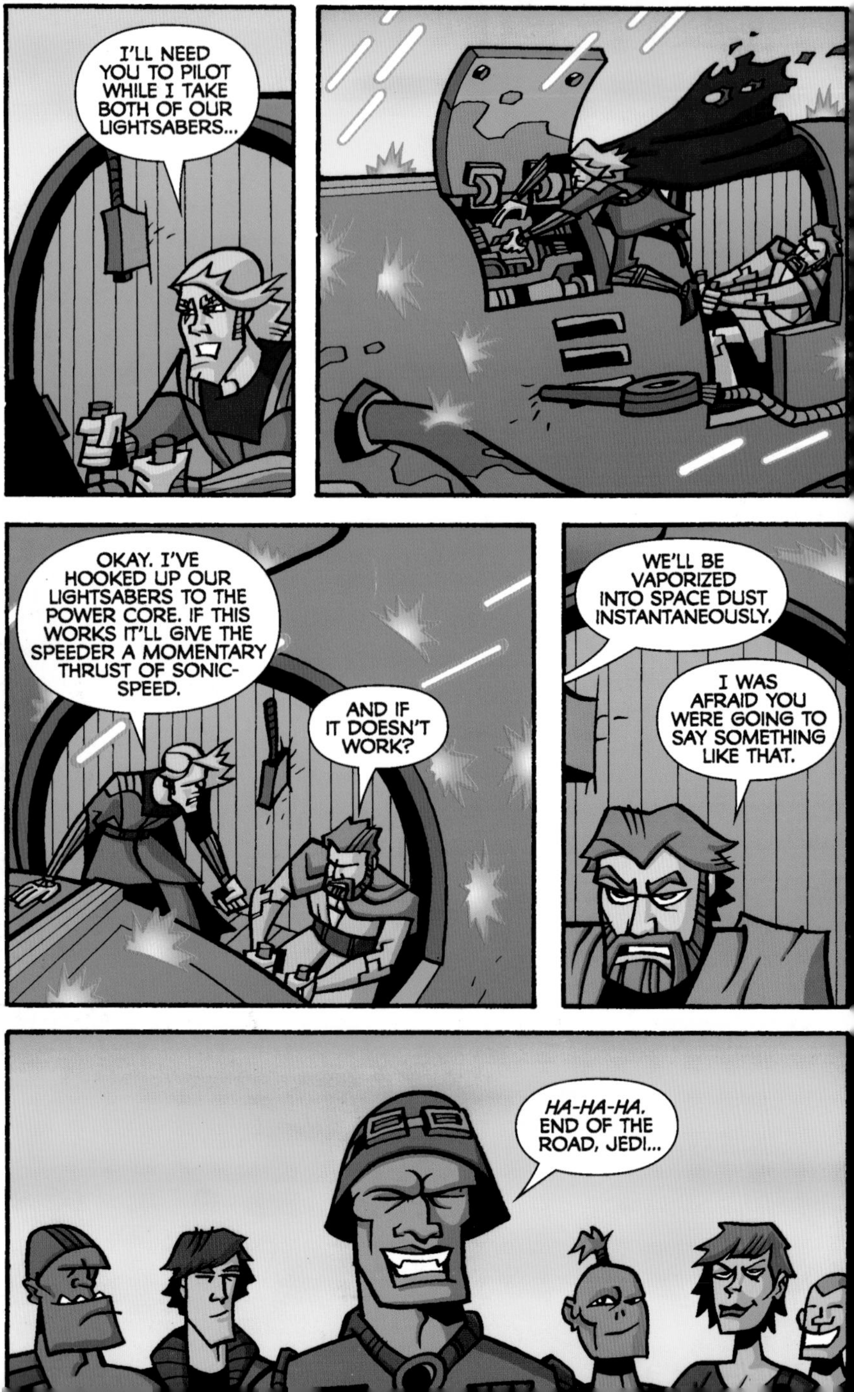
I'LL NEED YOU TO PILOT WHILE I TAKE BOTH OF OUR LIGHTSABERS...
OKAY. I'VE HOOKED UP OUR LIGHTSABERS TO THE POWER CORE. IF THIS WORKS IT'LL GIVE THE SPEEDER A MOMENTARY THRUST OF SONIC-SPEED.
AND IF IT DOESN'T WORK?
WE'LL BE VAPORIZED INTO SPACE DUST INSTANTANEOUSLY.
I WAS AFRAID YOU WERE GOING TO SAY SOMETHING LIKE THAT.
HA-HA-HA. END OF THE ROAD, JEDI...

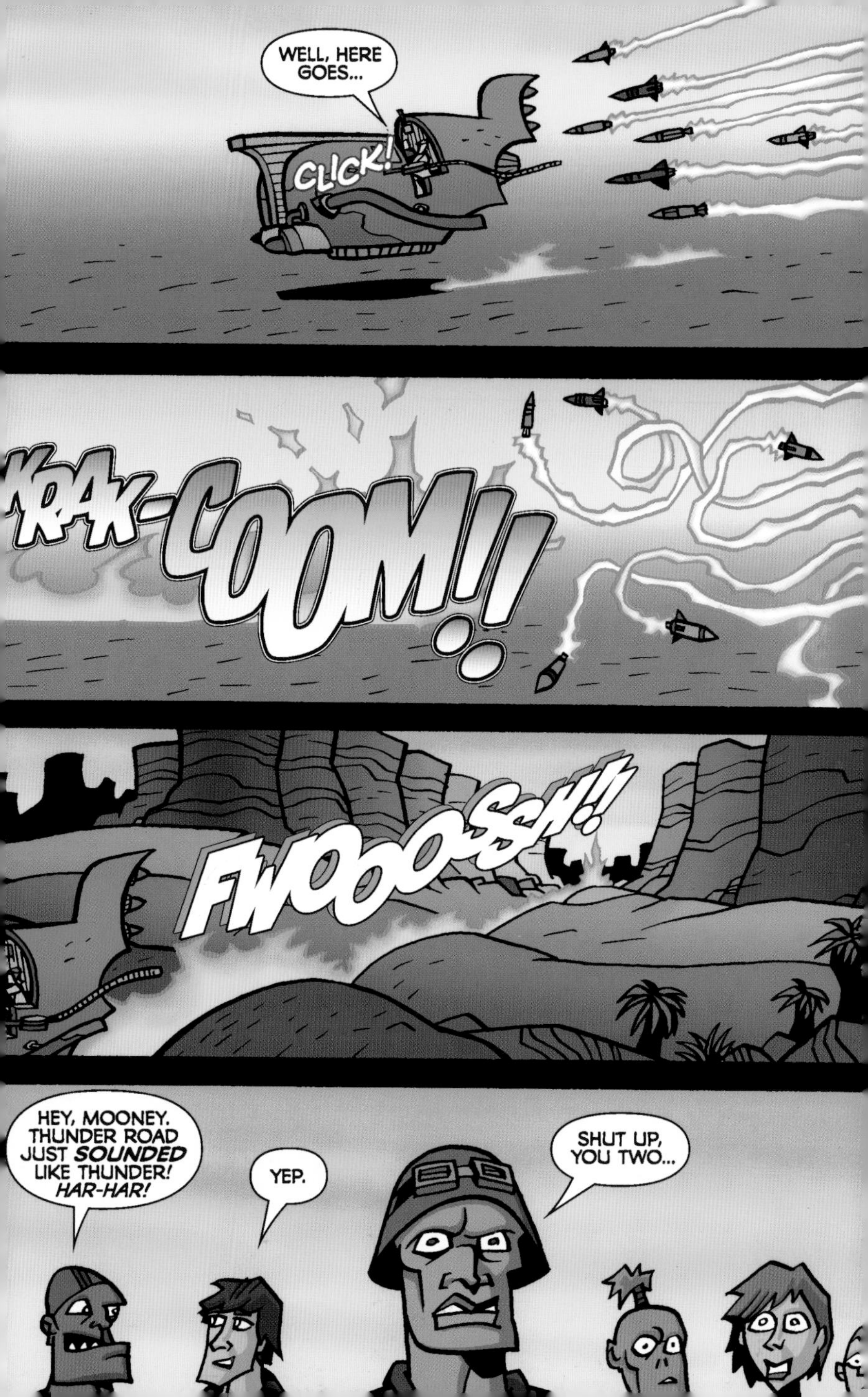
WELL, HERE GOES...
CL!CK!
KRAK-COOOM!!
FWOOOSSH!!
HEY, MOONEY. THUNDER ROAD JUST *SOUNDED* LIKE THUNDER! *HAR-HAR!*
YEP.
SHUT UP, YOU TWO...

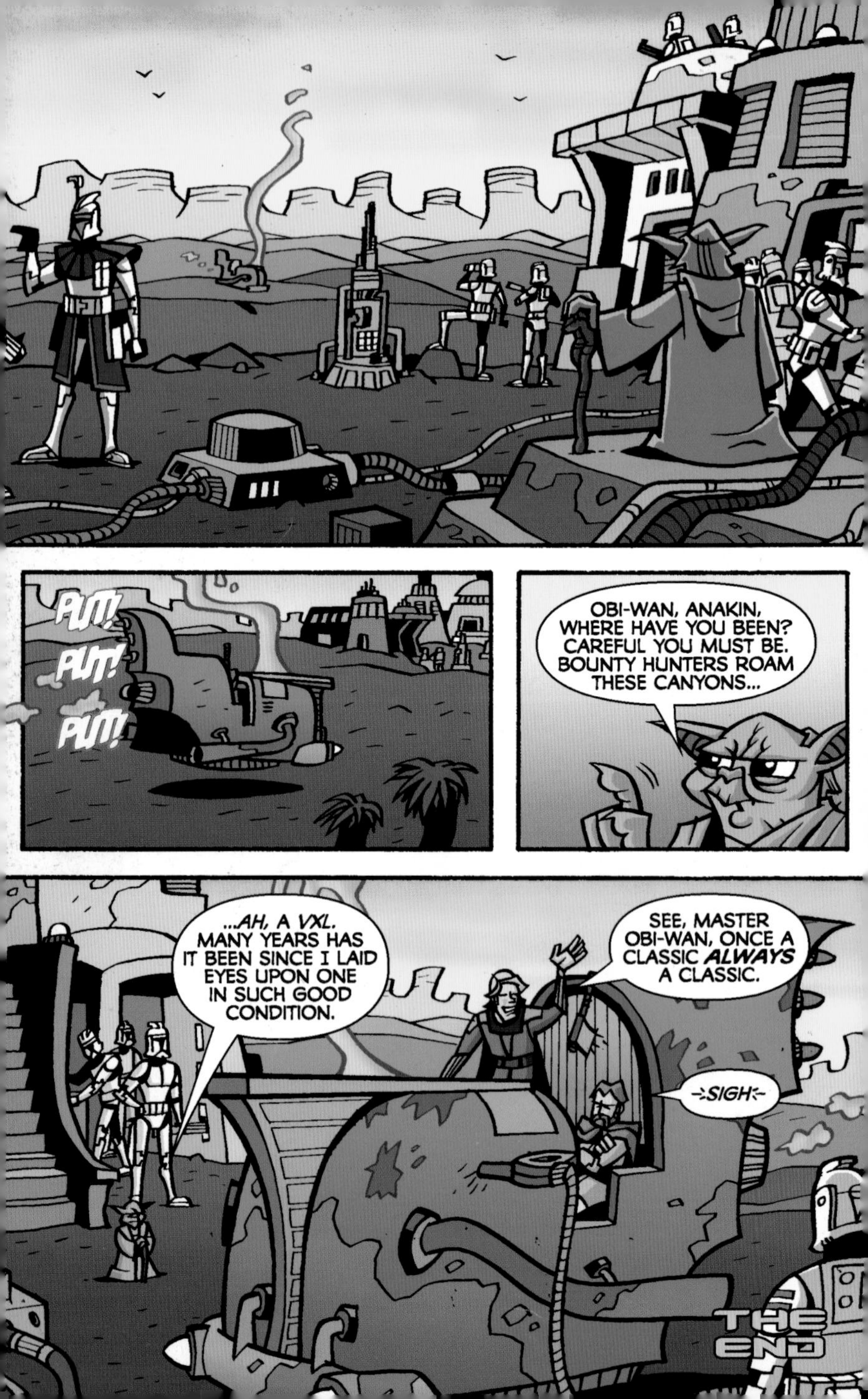
PUT!
PUT!
PUT!
OBI-WAN, ANAKIN, WHERE HAVE YOU BEEN? CAREFUL YOU MUST BE. BOUNTY HUNTERS ROAM THESE CANYONS...
...AH, A VXL. MANY YEARS HAS IT BEEN SINCE I LAID EYES UPON ONE IN SUCH GOOD CONDITION.
SEE, MASTER OBI-WAN, ONCE A CLASSIC *ALWAYS* A CLASSIC.
-SIGH-
THE END

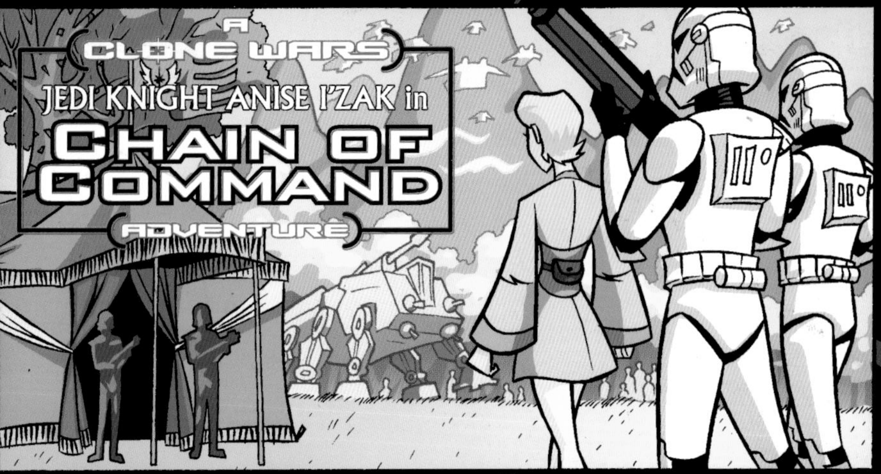
A
CLONE WARS
JEDI KNIGHT ANISE I'ZAK in
CHAIN OF COMMAND
ADVENTURE

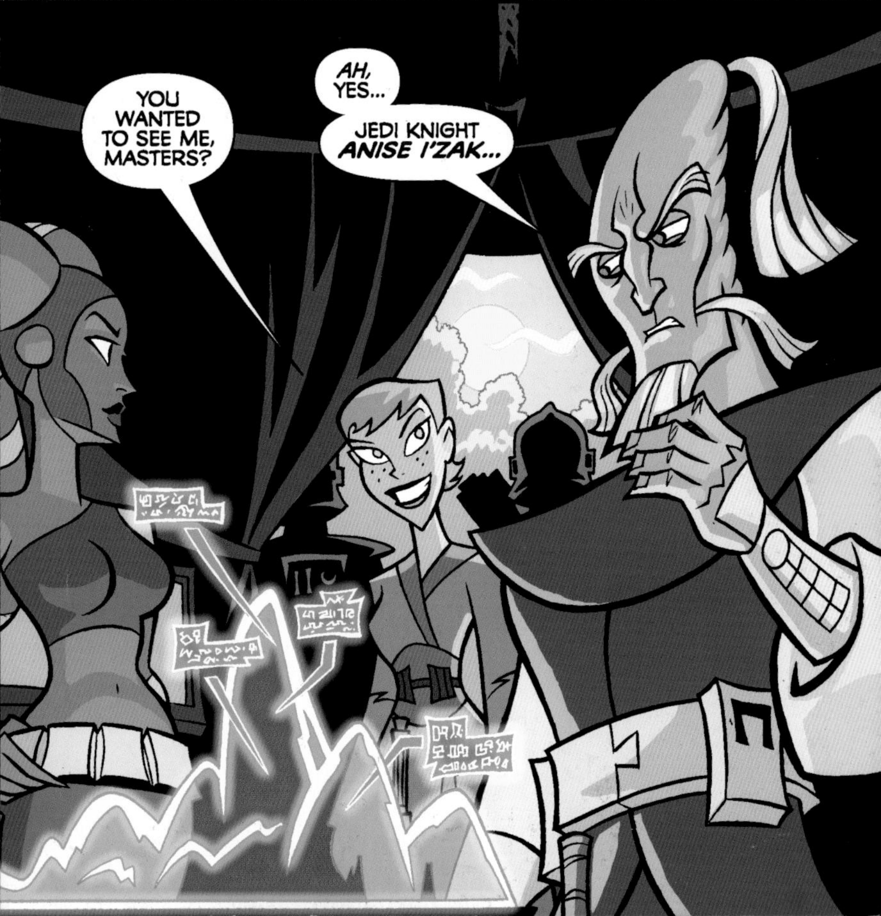
YOU WANTED TO SEE ME, MASTERS?
AH, YES...
JEDI KNIGHT *ANISE I'ZAK...*

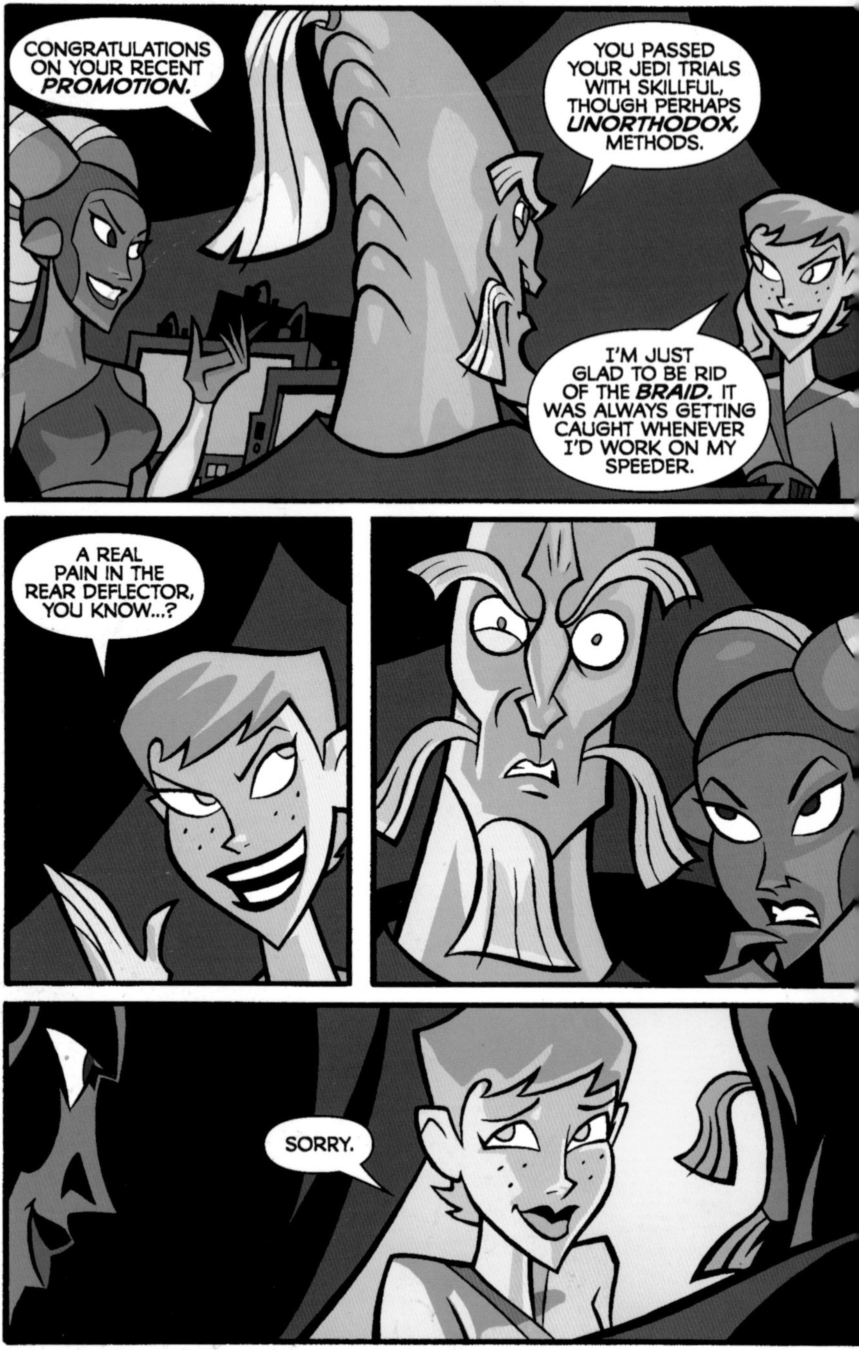
CONGRATULATIONS ON YOUR RECENT PROMOTION.
YOU PASSED YOUR JEDI TRIALS WITH SKILLFUL, THOUGH PERHAPS UNORTHODOX, METHODS.
I'M JUST GLAD TO BE RID OF THE BRAID. IT WAS ALWAYS GETTING CAUGHT WHENEVER I'D WORK ON MY SPEEDER.
A REAL PAIN IN THE REAR DEFLECTOR, YOU KNOW...?
SORRY.

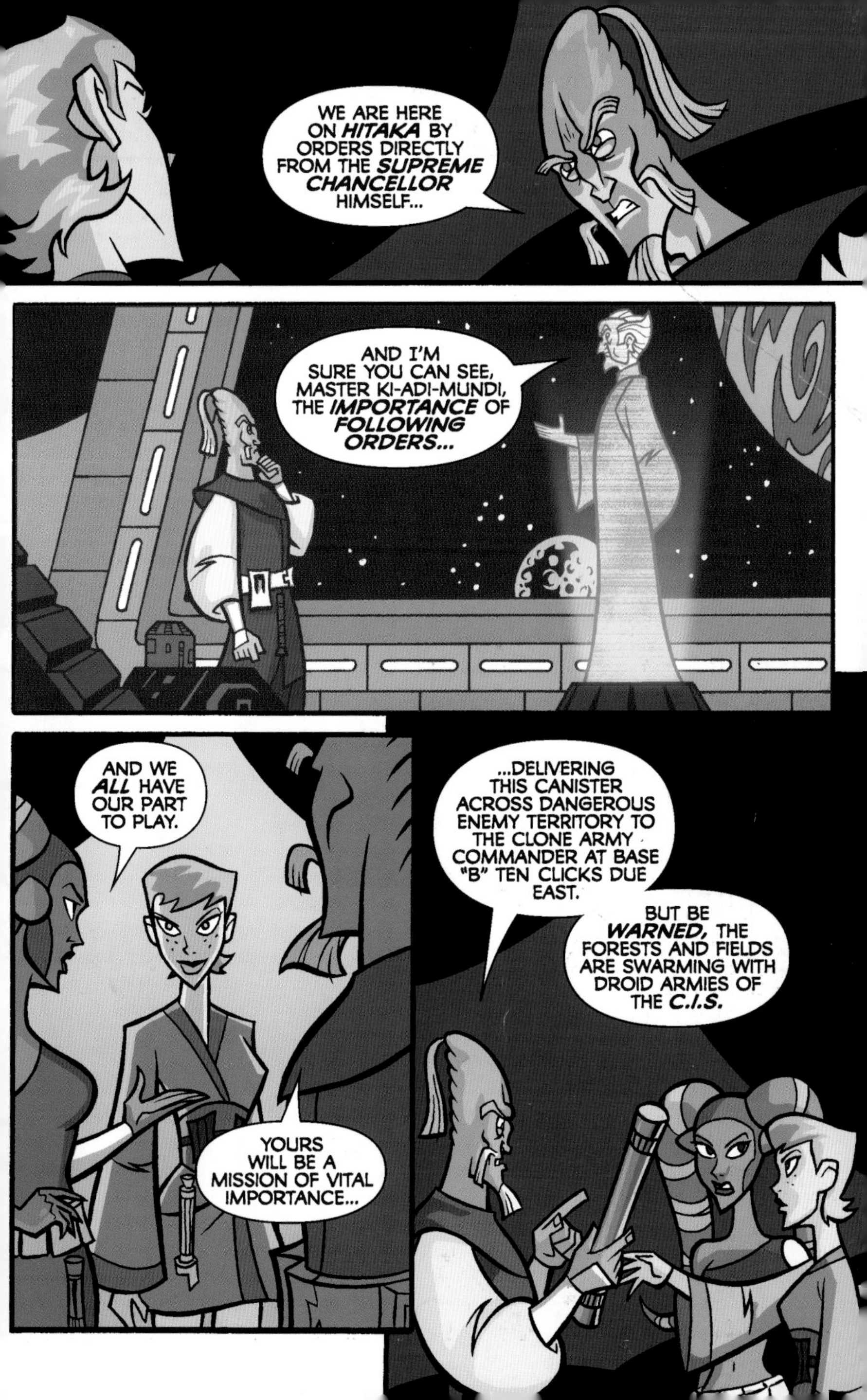
WE ARE HERE ON HITAKA BY ORDERS DIRECTLY FROM THE SUPREME CHANCELLOR HIMSELF...
AND I'M SURE YOU CAN SEE, MASTER KI-ADI-MUNDI, THE IMPORTANCE OF FOLLOWING ORDERS...
AND WE ALL HAVE OUR PART TO PLAY.
YOURS WILL BE A MISSION OF VITAL IMPORTANCE...
...DELIVERING THIS CANISTER ACROSS DANGEROUS ENEMY TERRITORY TO THE CLONE ARMY COMMANDER AT BASE "B" TEN CLICKS DUE EAST.
BUT BE WARNED, THE FORESTS AND FIELDS ARE SWARMING WITH DROID ARMIES OF THE C.I.S.

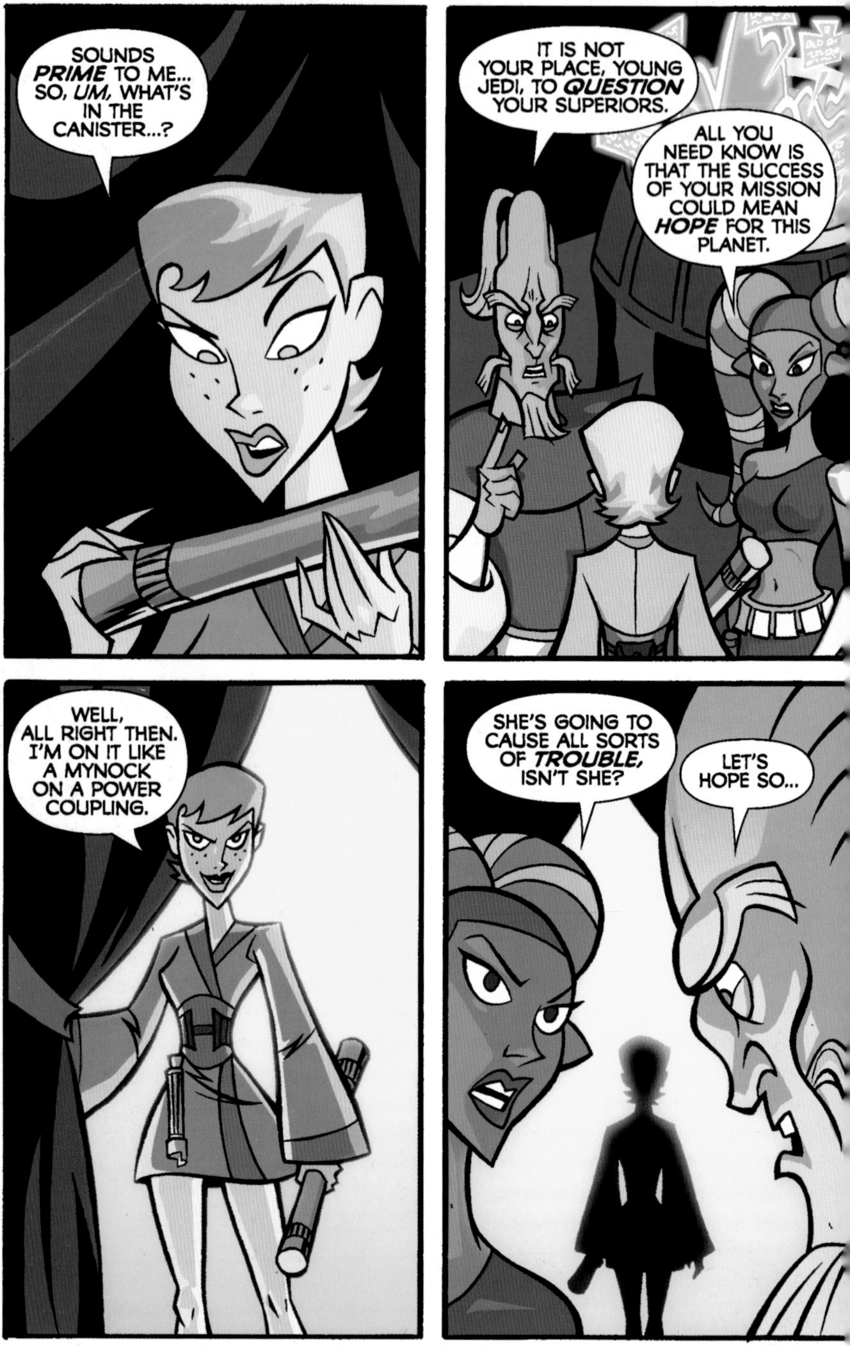
SOUNDS PRIME TO ME... SO, UM, WHAT'S IN THE CANISTER...?
IT IS NOT YOUR PLACE, YOUNG JEDI, TO QUESTION YOUR SUPERIORS.
ALL YOU NEED KNOW IS THAT THE SUCCESS OF YOUR MISSION COULD MEAN HOPE FOR THIS PLANET.
WELL, ALL RIGHT THEN. I'M ON IT LIKE A MYNOCK ON A POWER COUPLING.
SHE'S GOING TO CAUSE ALL SORTS OF TROUBLE, ISN'T SHE?
LET'S HOPE SO...

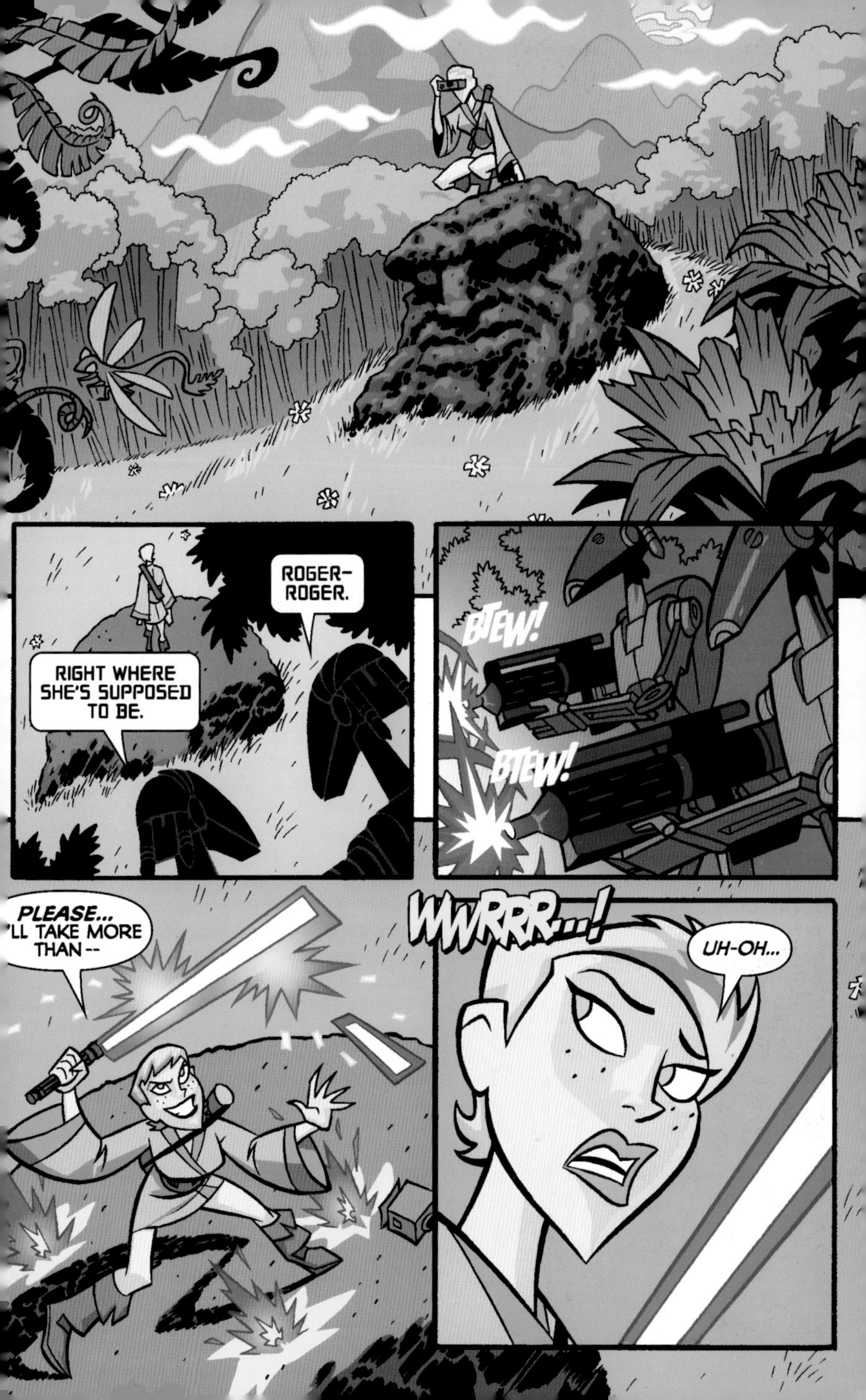
RIGHT WHERE SHE'S SUPPOSED TO BE.
ROGER-ROGER.
BTEW!
BTEW!
PLEASE... 'LL TAKE MORE THAN --
WWRRR...!
UH-OH...

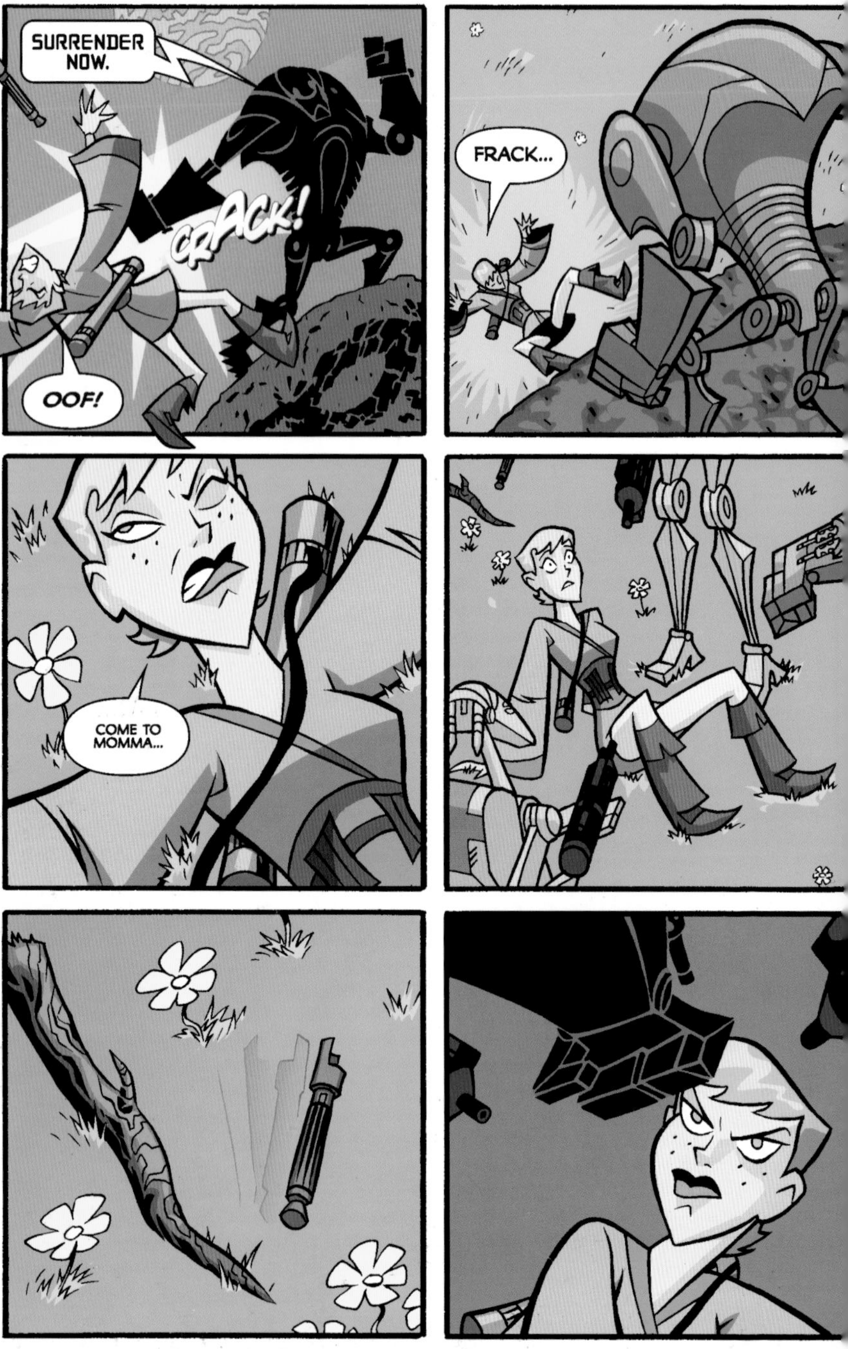
SURRENDER NOW.
CRACK!
OOF!
FRACK...
COME TO MOMMA...

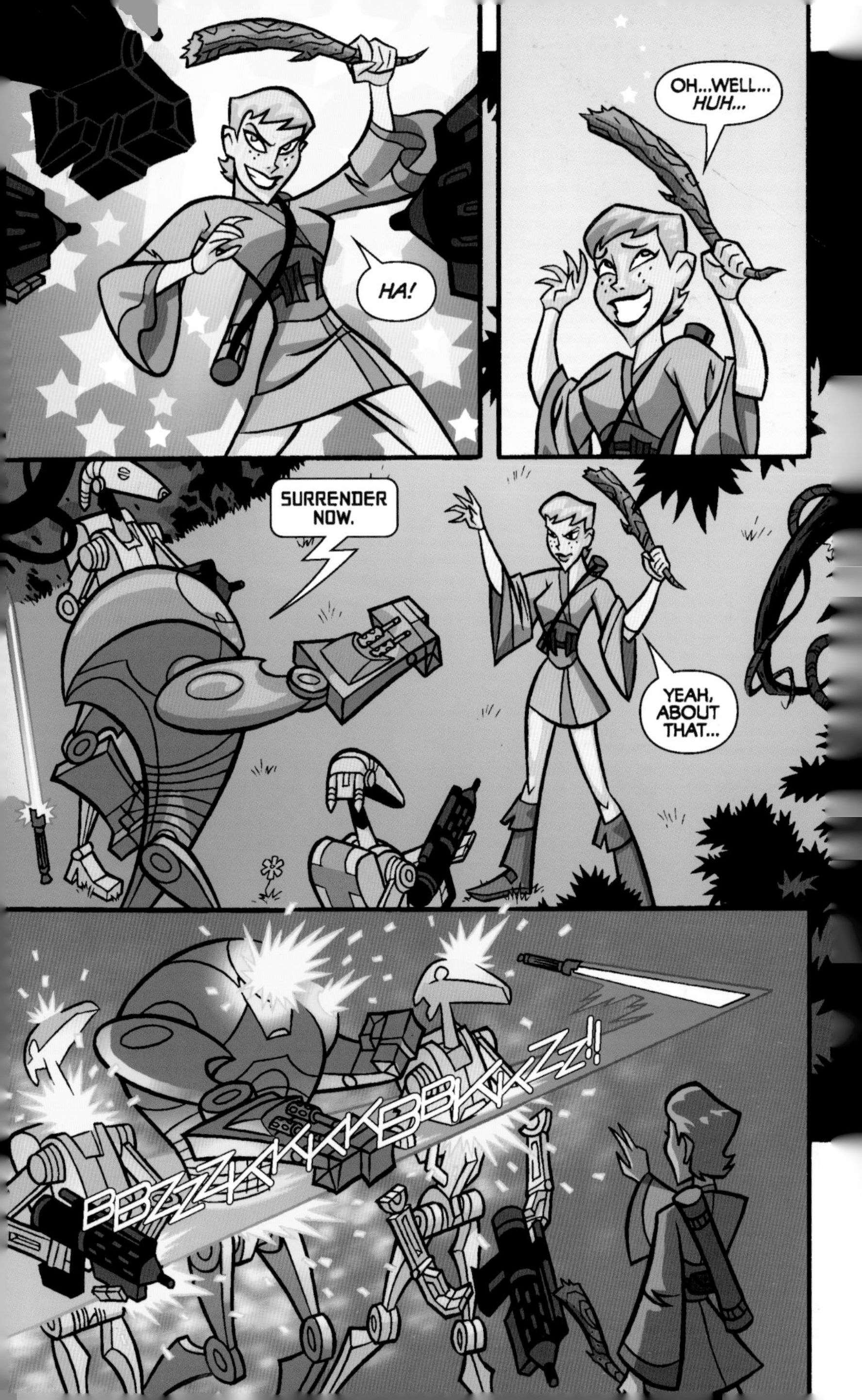
HA!
OH...WELL... HUH...
SURRENDER NOW.
YEAH, ABOUT THAT...
BBZZZKKKKKBBBKKZZ!!

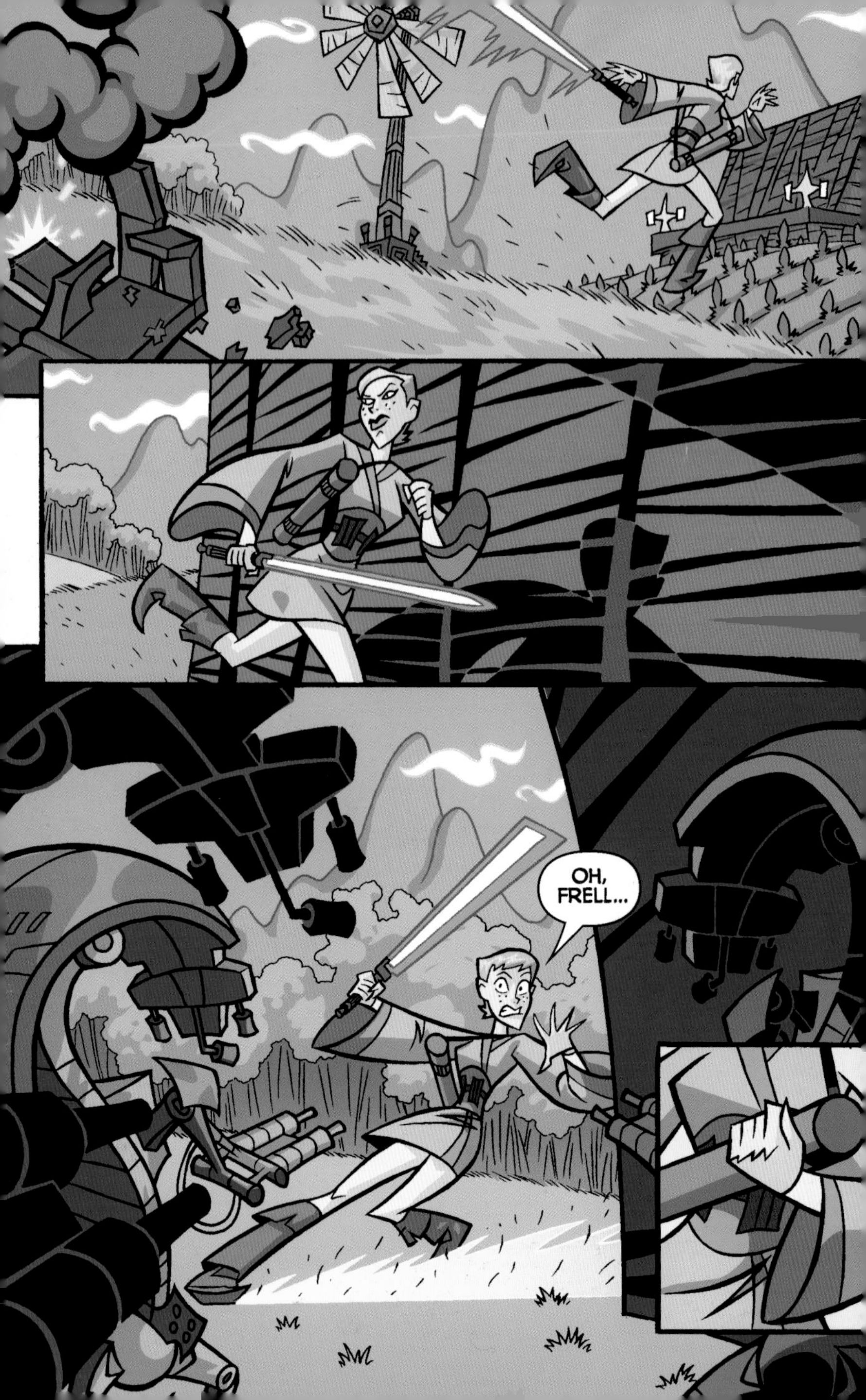
OH, FRELL...

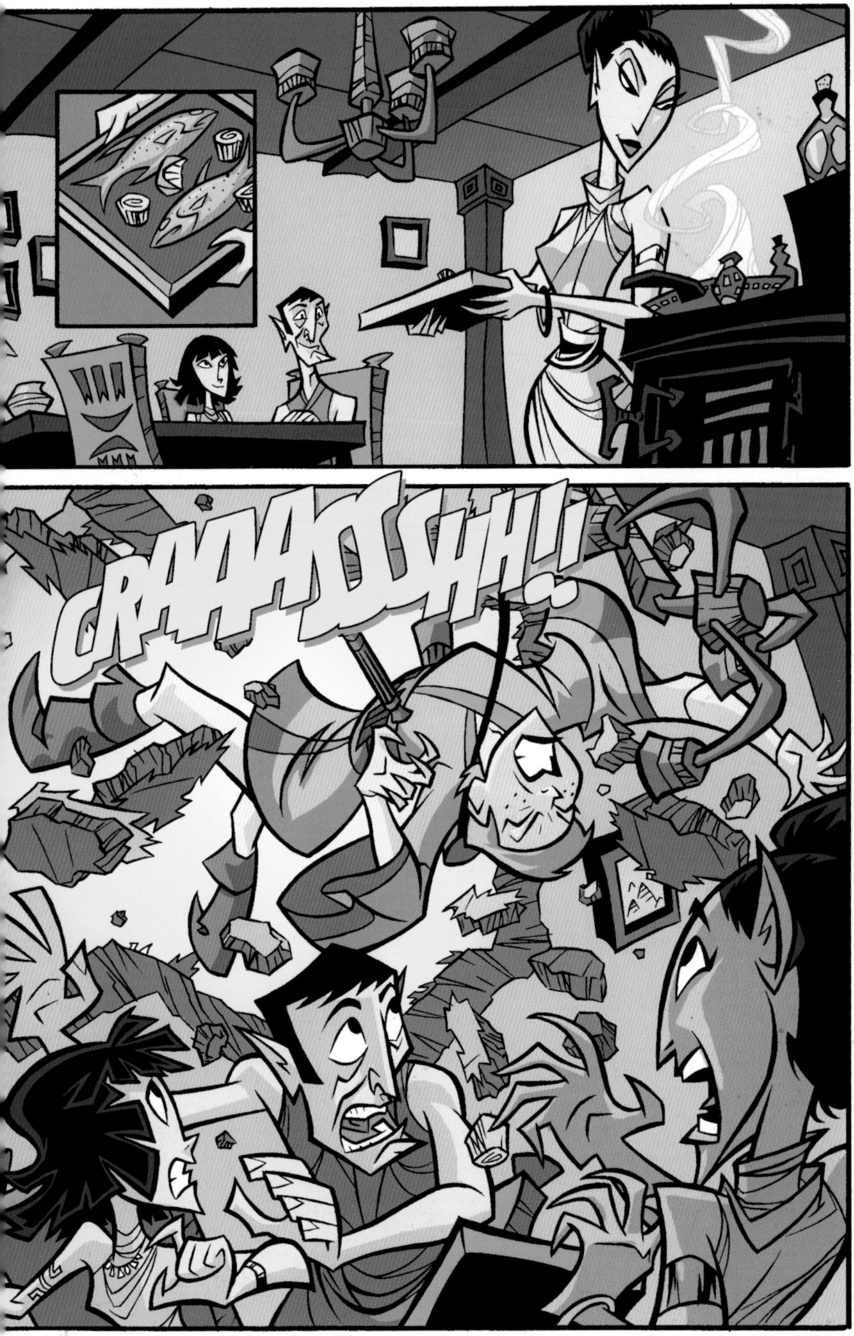
CRAAASSH!!

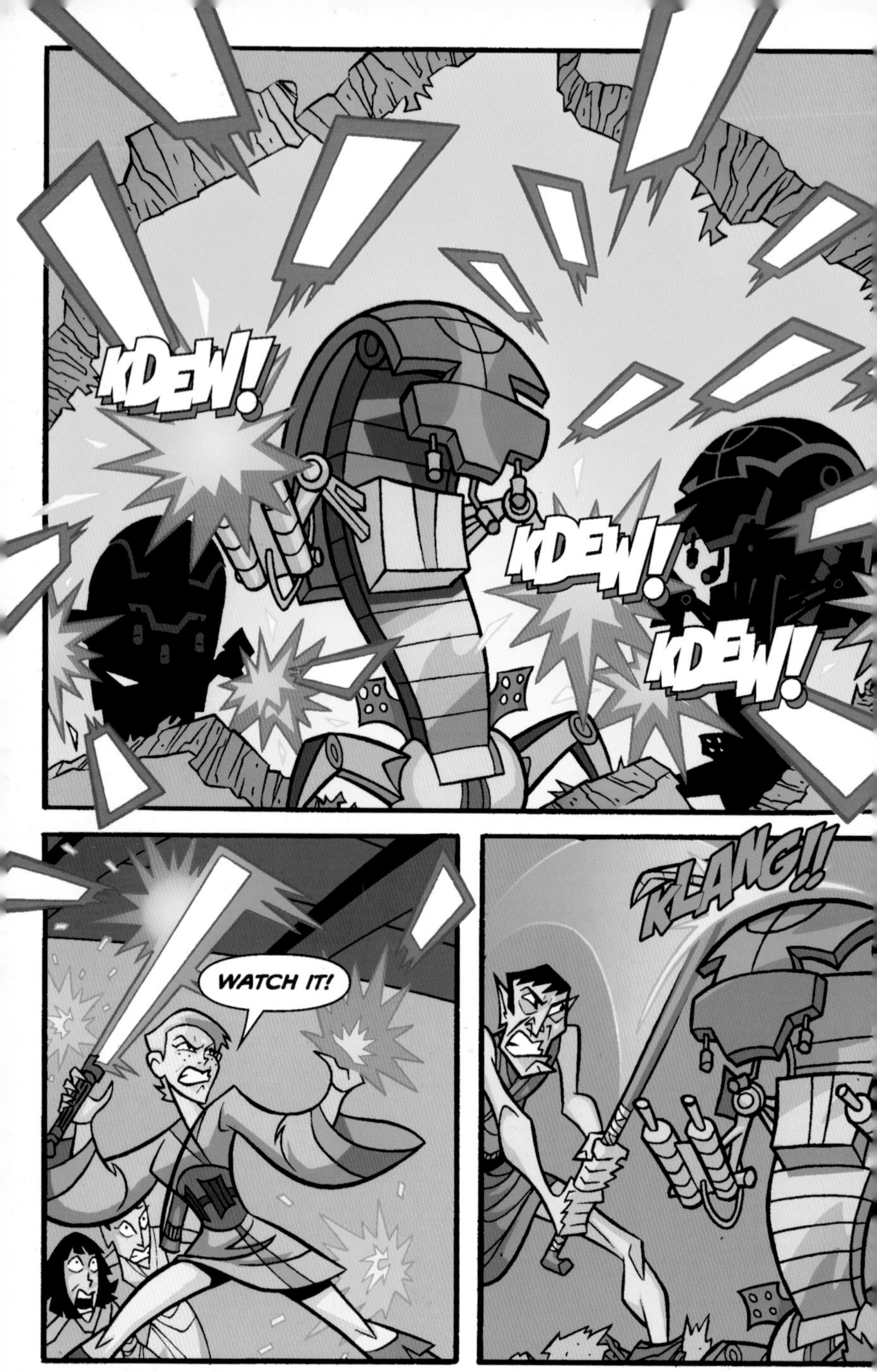

KDEW!
KDEW!
KDEW!
WATCH IT!
KLANG!!

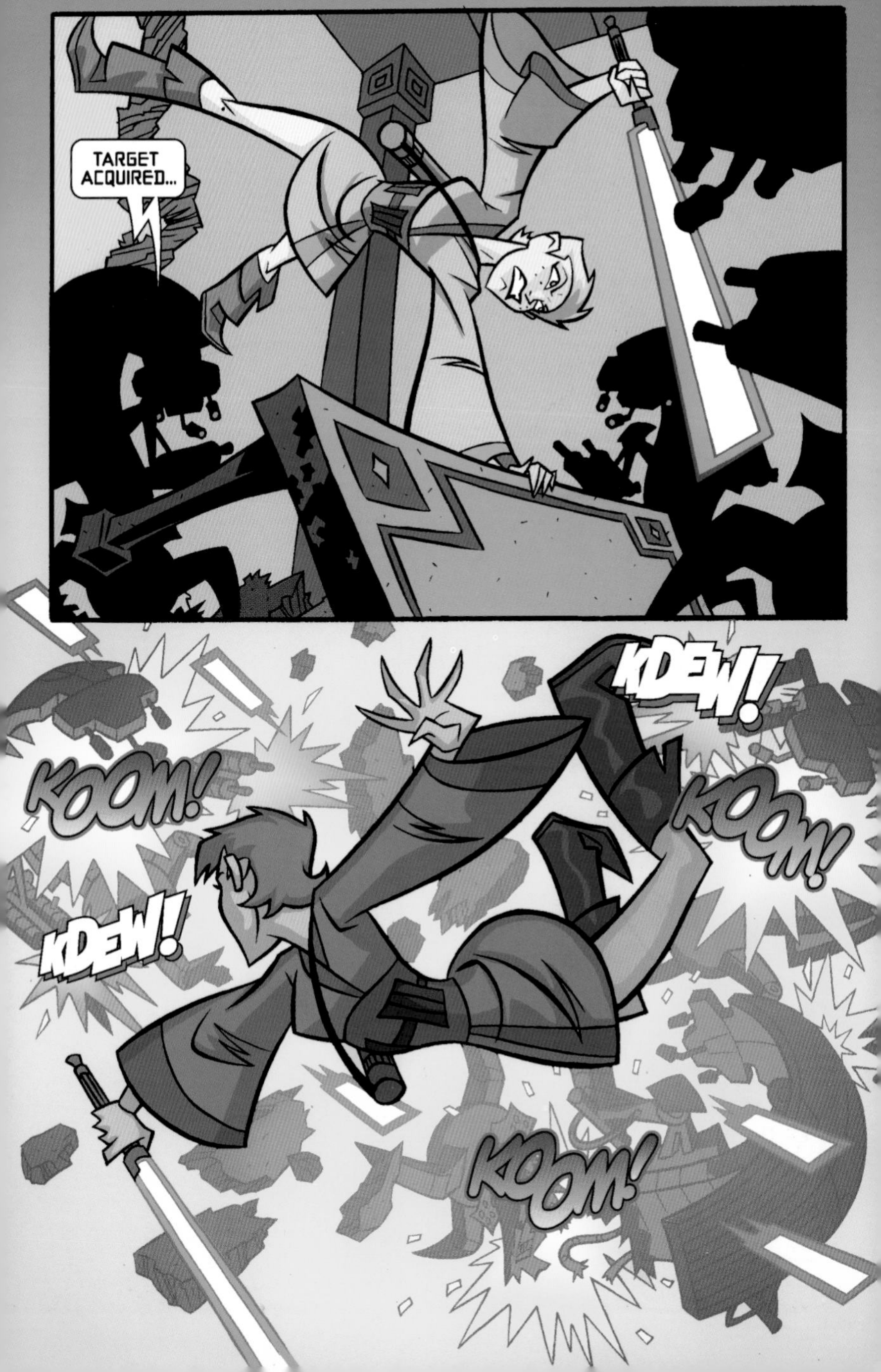
TARGET ACQUIRED...
KDEW!
KOOM!
KOOM!
KDEW!
KOOM!

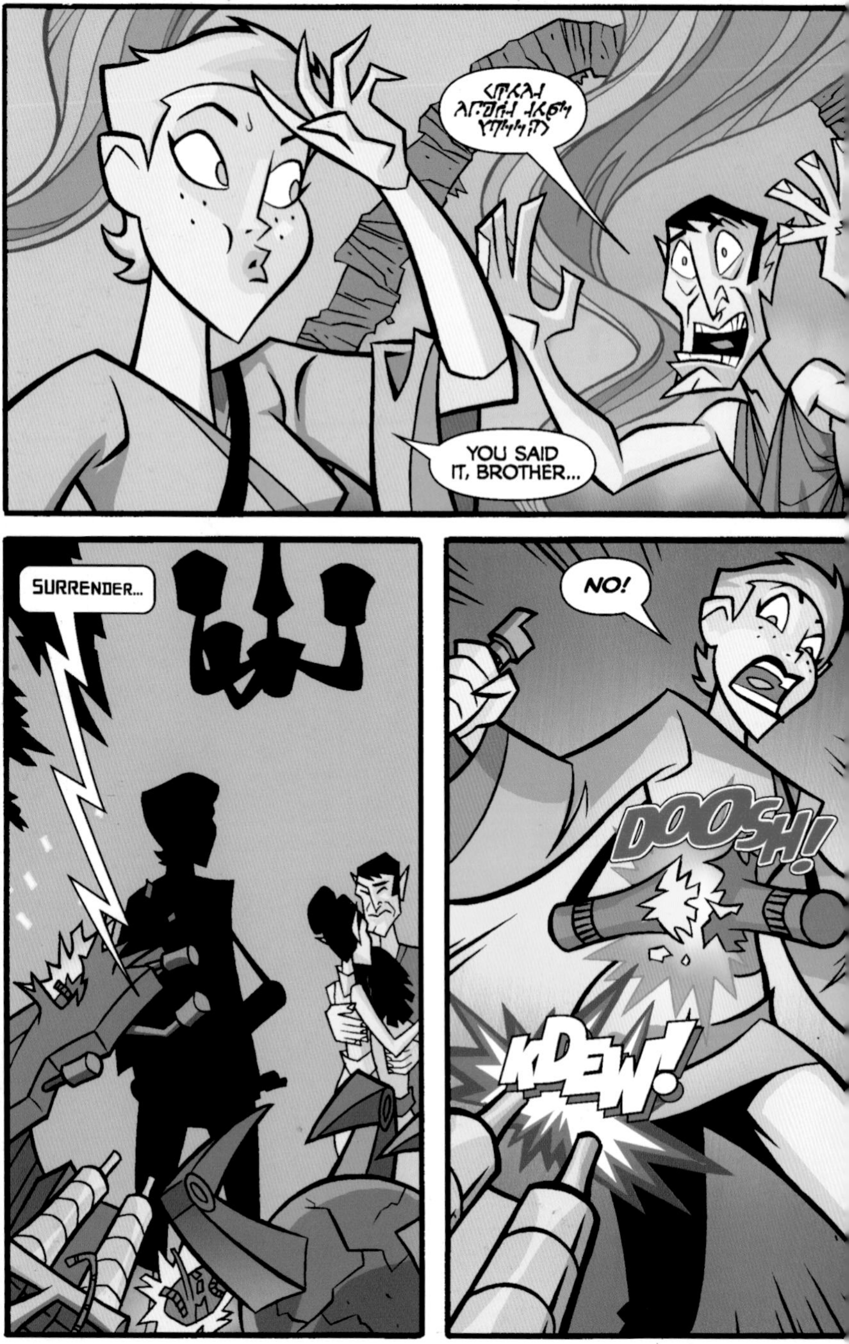
YOU SAID IT, BROTHER...
SURRENDER...
NO!
DOOSH!
KDEW!

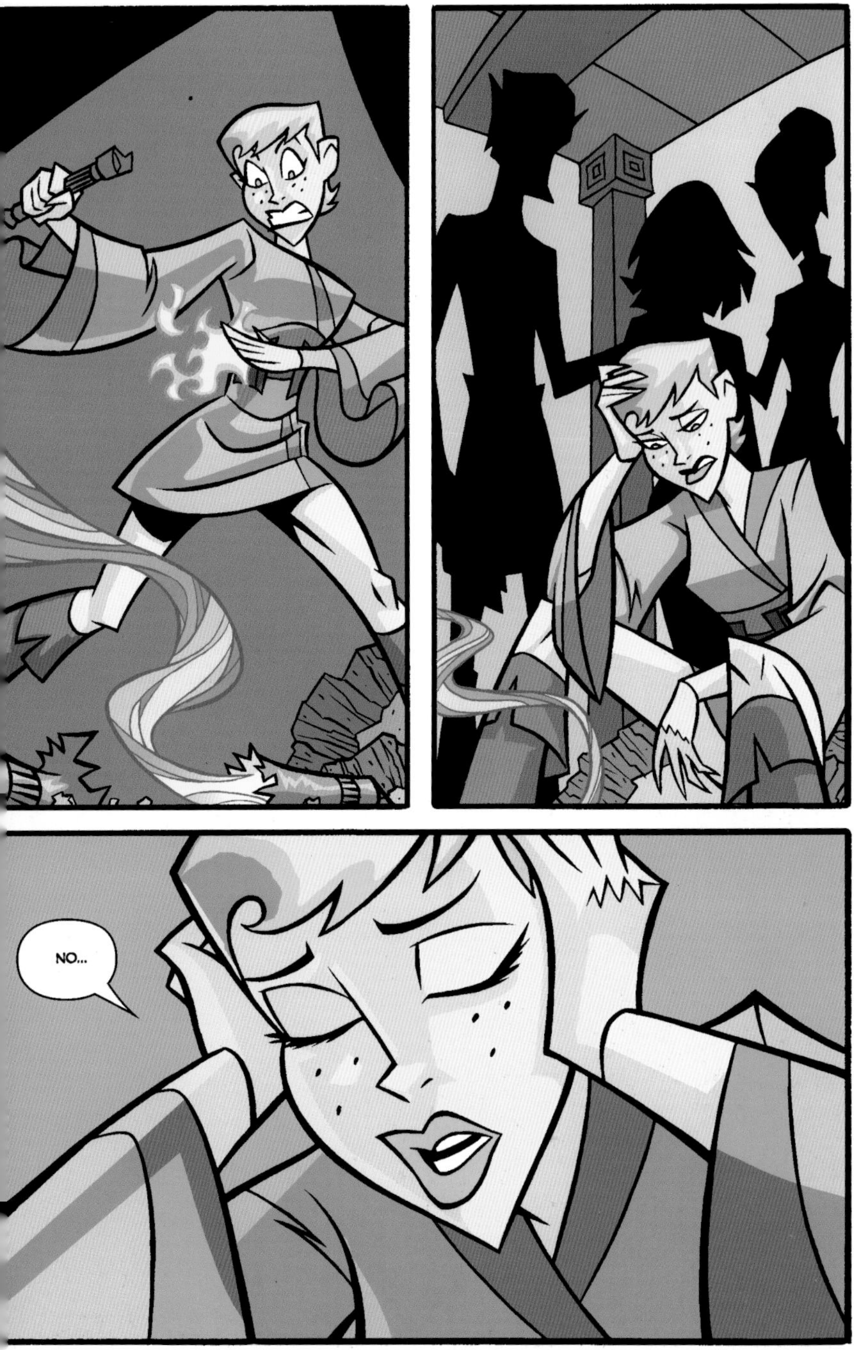
NO...

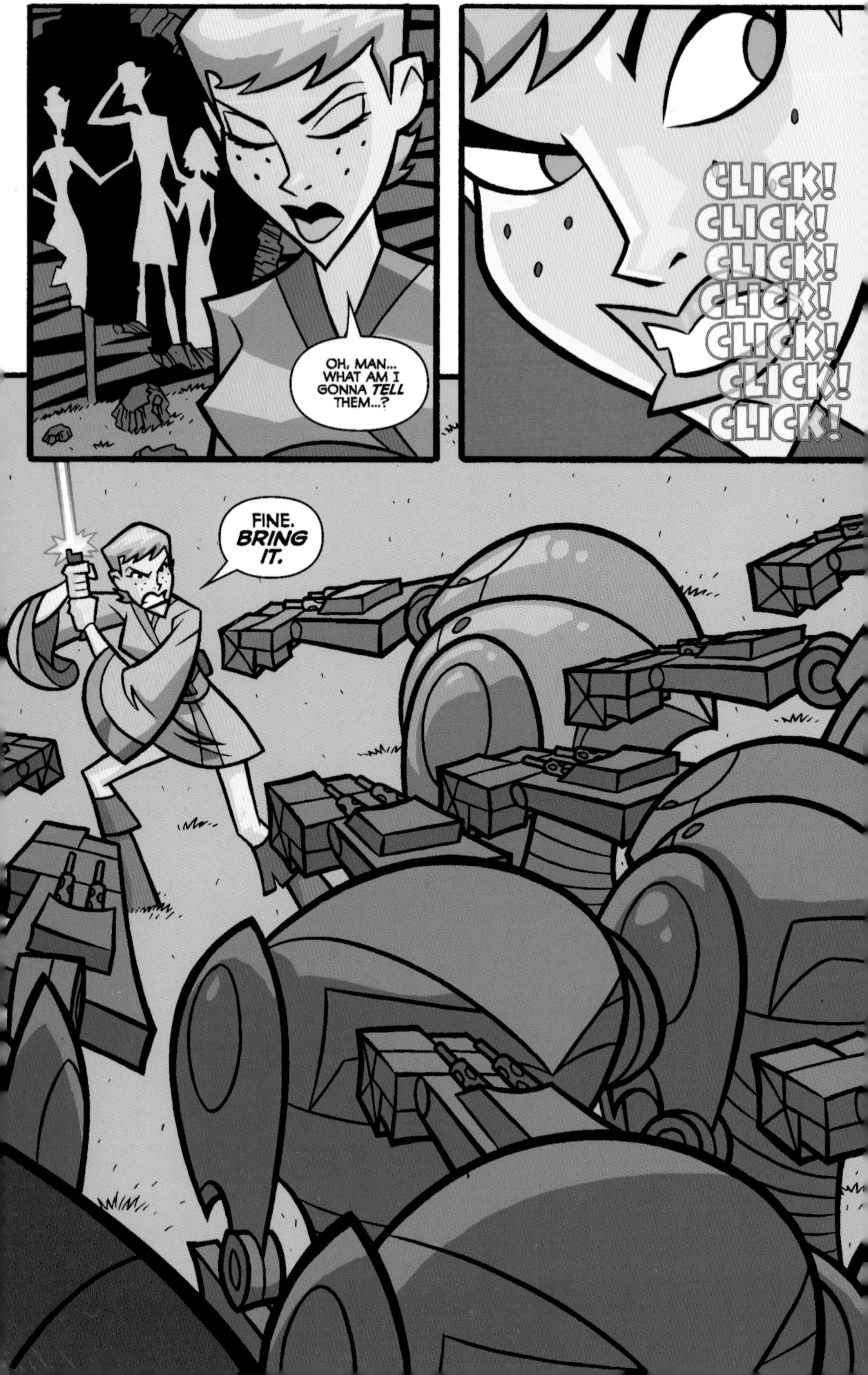
OH, MAN... WHAT AM I GONNA *TELL* THEM...?
CLICK! CLICK! CLICK! CLICK! CLICK! CLICK! CLICK!
FINE. *BRING IT.*

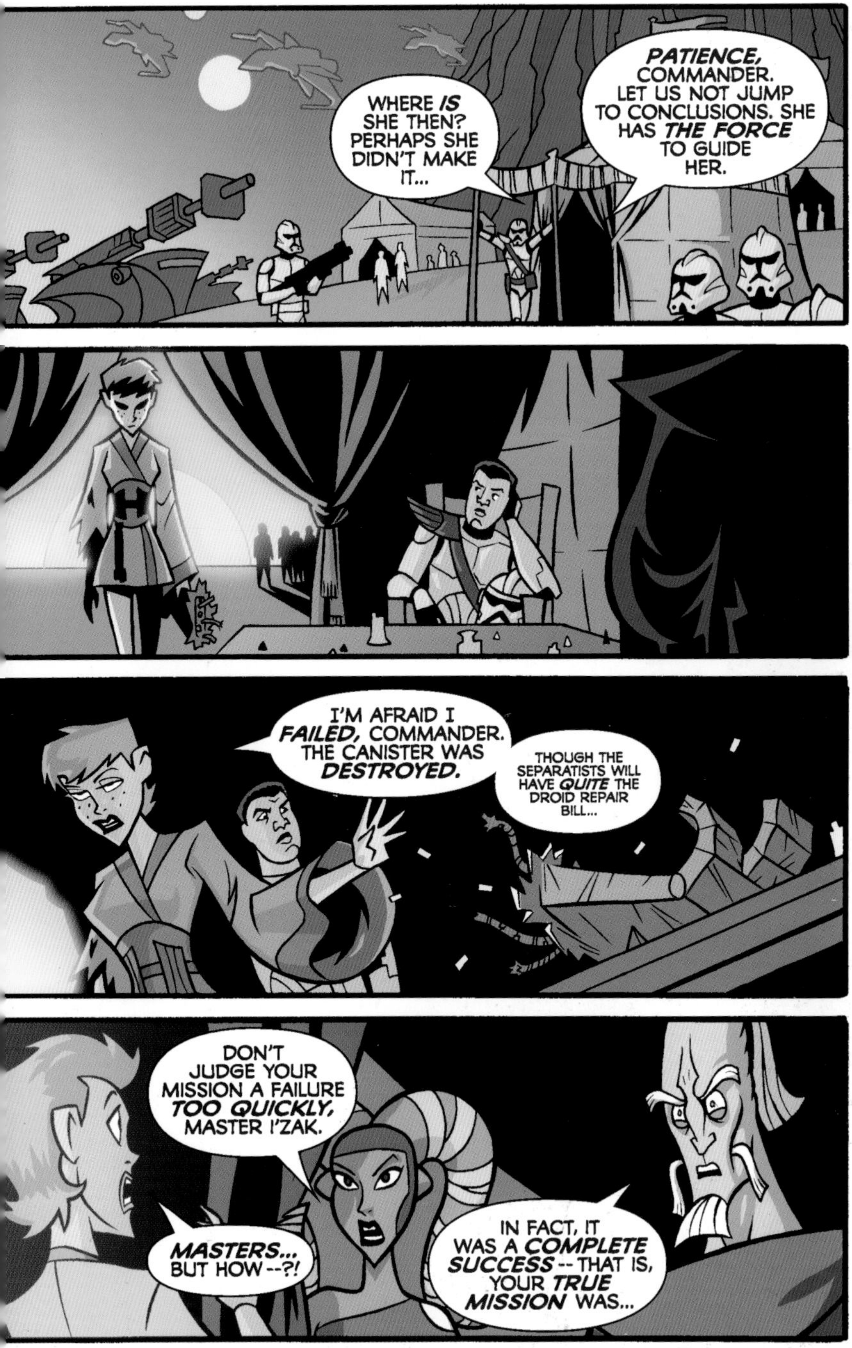
WHERE *IS* SHE THEN? PERHAPS SHE DIDN'T MAKE IT...
PATIENCE, COMMANDER. LET US NOT JUMP TO CONCLUSIONS. SHE HAS *THE FORCE* TO GUIDE HER.
I'M AFRAID I *FAILED,* COMMANDER. THE CANISTER WAS *DESTROYED.*
THOUGH THE SEPARATISTS WILL HAVE *QUITE* THE DROID REPAIR BILL...
DON'T JUDGE YOUR MISSION A FAILURE *TOO QUICKLY,* MASTER I'ZAK.
MASTERS... BUT HOW--?!
IN FACT, IT WAS A *COMPLETE SUCCESS*-- THAT IS, YOUR *TRUE MISSION* WAS...

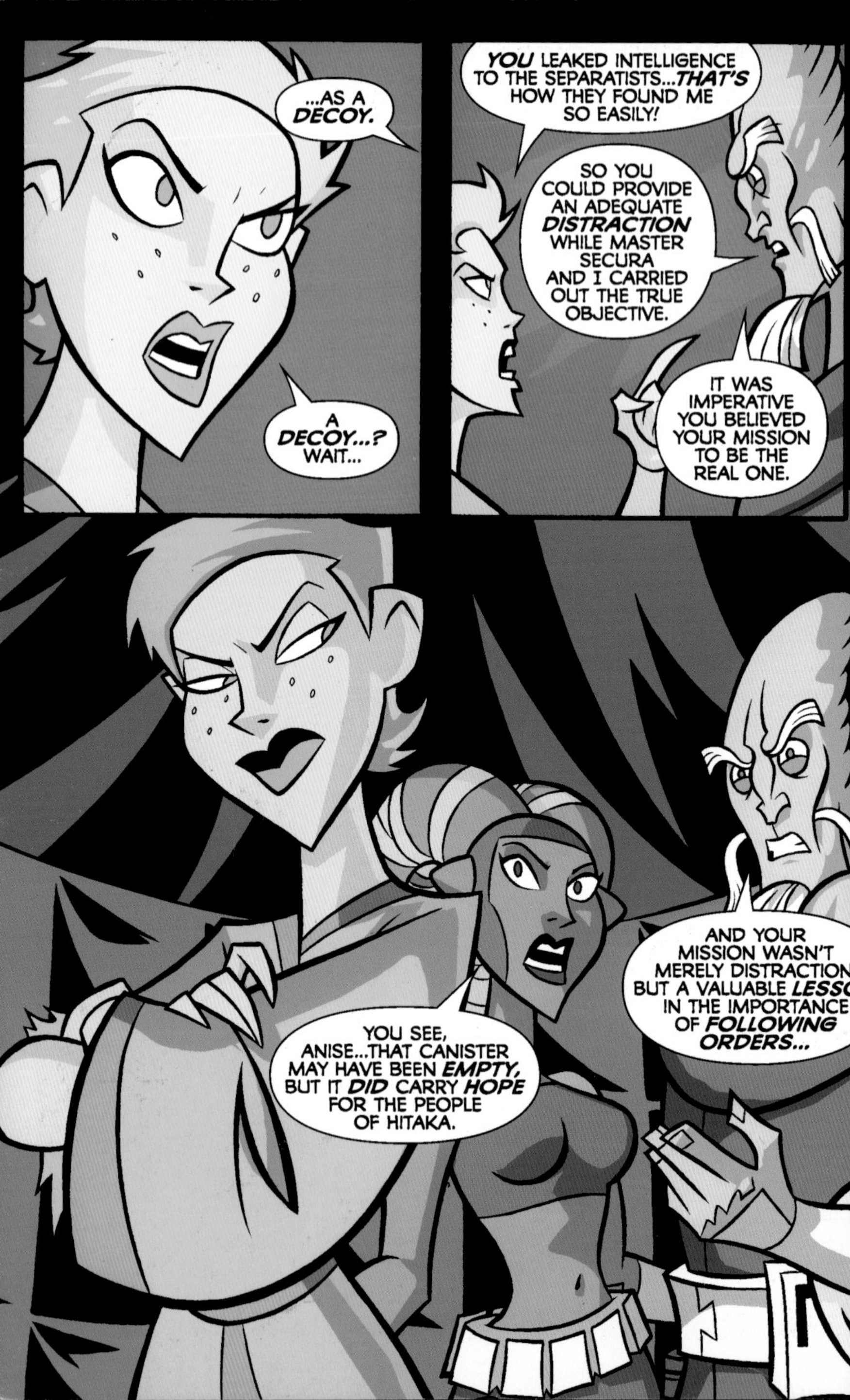
...AS A DECOY.
A DECOY...? WAIT...
YOU LEAKED INTELLIGENCE TO THE SEPARATISTS...THAT'S HOW THEY FOUND ME SO EASILY!
SO YOU COULD PROVIDE AN ADEQUATE DISTRACTION WHILE MASTER SECURA AND I CARRIED OUT THE TRUE OBJECTIVE.
IT WAS IMPERATIVE YOU BELIEVED YOUR MISSION TO BE THE REAL ONE.
AND YOUR MISSION WASN'T MERELY DISTRACTION BUT A VALUABLE LESSO IN THE IMPORTANCE OF FOLLOWING ORDERS...
YOU SEE, ANISE...THAT CANISTER MAY HAVE BEEN EMPTY, BUT IT DID CARRY HOPE FOR THE PEOPLE OF HITAKA.

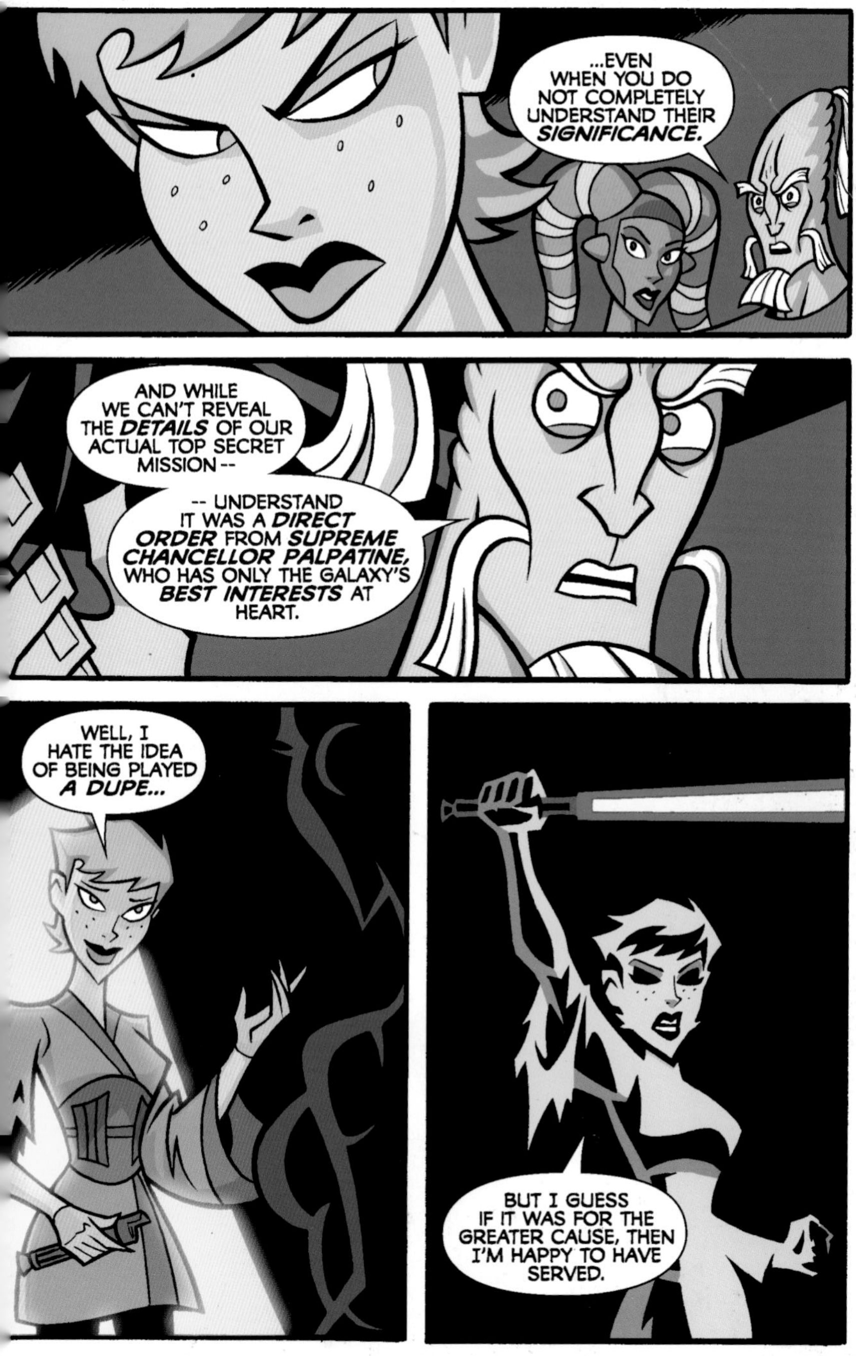
...EVEN WHEN YOU DO NOT COMPLETELY UNDERSTAND THEIR *SIGNIFICANCE.*
AND WHILE WE CAN'T REVEAL THE *DETAILS* OF OUR ACTUAL TOP SECRET MISSION --
-- UNDERSTAND IT WAS A *DIRECT ORDER* FROM *SUPREME CHANCELLOR PALPATINE,* WHO HAS ONLY THE GALAXY'S *BEST INTERESTS* AT HEART.
WELL, I HATE THE IDEA OF BEING PLAYED *A DUPE...*
BUT I GUESS IF IT WAS FOR THE GREATER CAUSE, THEN I'M HAPPY TO HAVE SERVED.

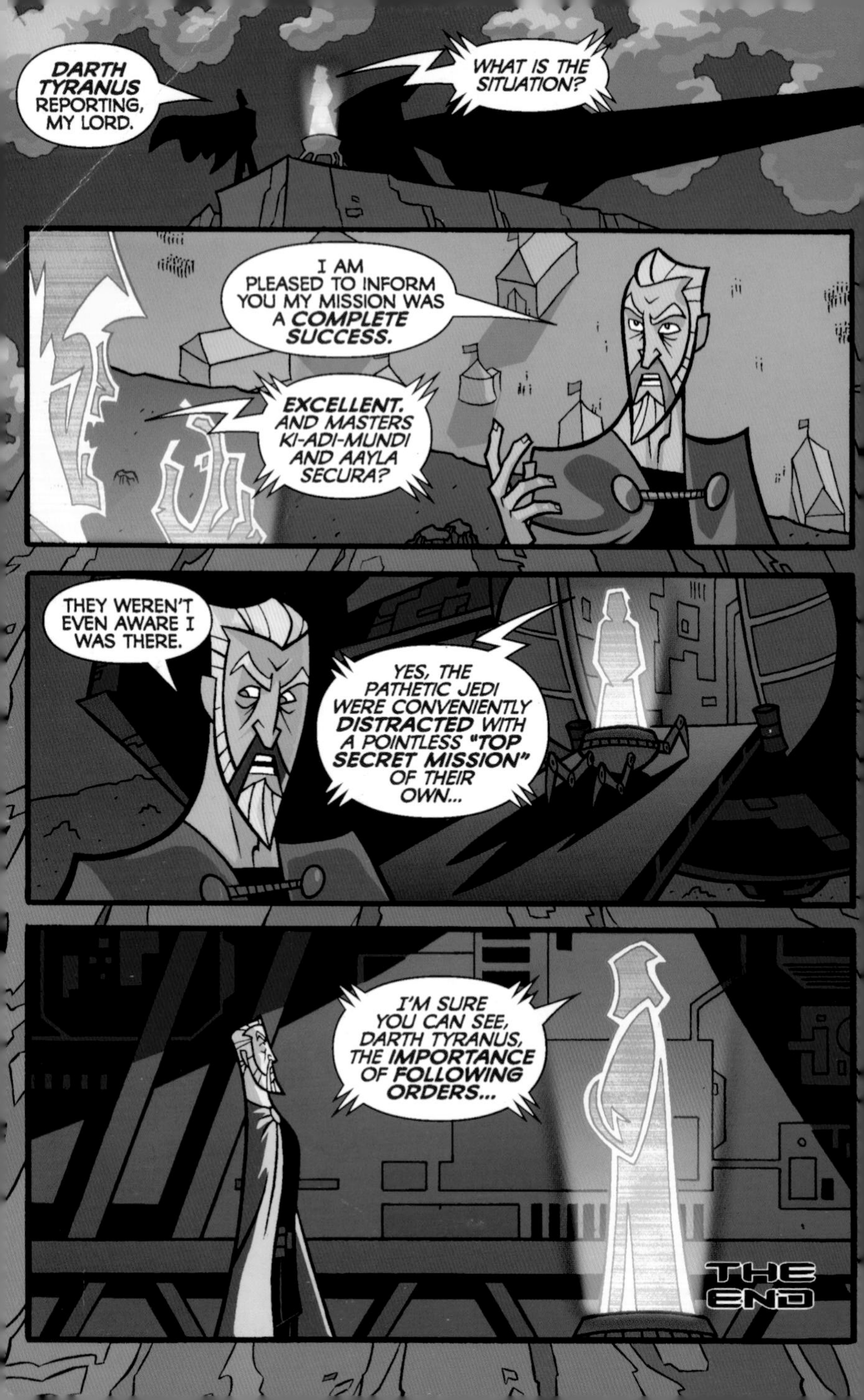
DARTH TYRANUS REPORTING, MY LORD.
WHAT IS THE SITUATION?
I AM PLEASED TO INFORM YOU MY MISSION WAS A COMPLETE SUCCESS.
EXCELLENT. AND MASTERS KI-ADI-MUNDI AND AAYLA SECURA?
THEY WEREN'T EVEN AWARE I WAS THERE.
YES, THE PATHETIC JEDI WERE CONVENIENTLY DISTRACTED WITH A POINTLESS "TOP SECRET MISSION" OF THEIR OWN...
I'M SURE YOU CAN SEE, DARTH TYRANUS, THE IMPORTANCE OF FOLLOWING ORDERS...
THE END

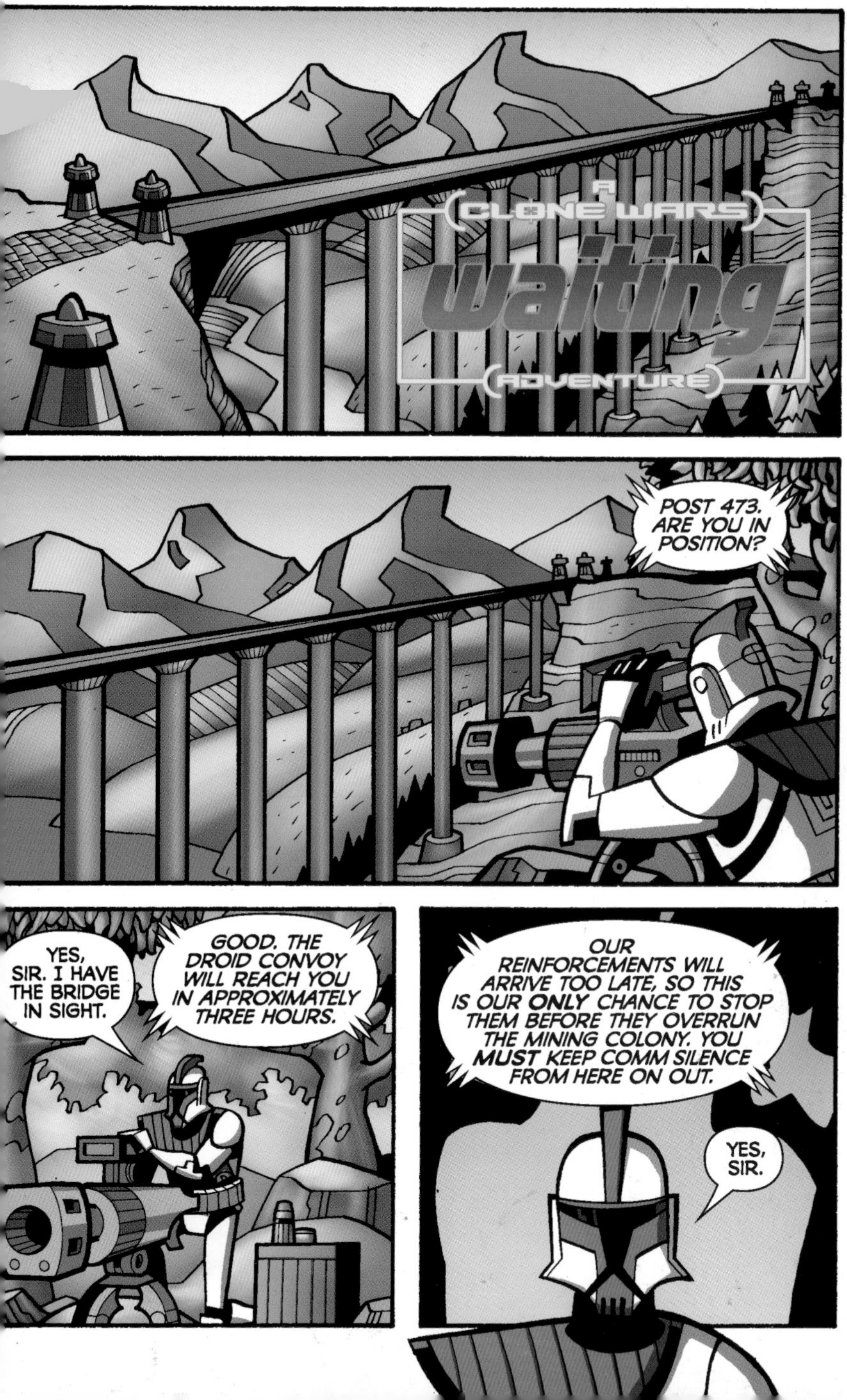
A
CLONE WARS
waiting
ADVENTURE
POST 473. ARE YOU IN POSITION?
YES, SIR. I HAVE THE BRIDGE IN SIGHT.
GOOD. THE DROID CONVOY WILL REACH YOU IN APPROXIMATELY THREE HOURS.
OUR REINFORCEMENTS WILL ARRIVE TOO LATE, SO THIS IS OUR ONLY CHANCE TO STOP THEM BEFORE THEY OVERRUN THE MINING COLONY. YOU MUST KEEP COMM SILENCE FROM HERE ON OUT.
YES, SIR.

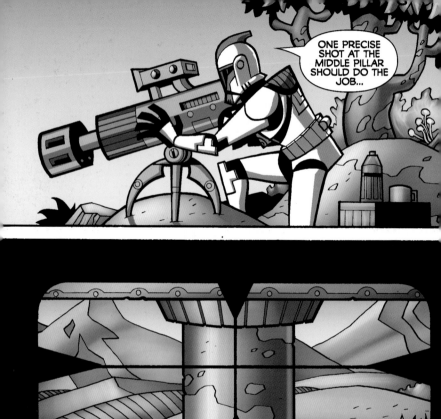

ONE PRECISE SHOT AT THE MIDDLE PILLAR SHOULD DO THE JOB...

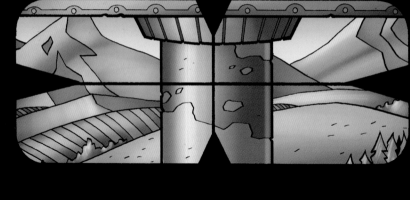

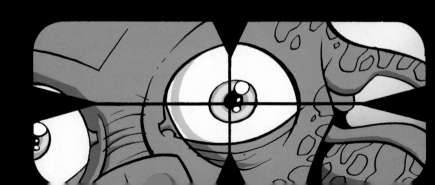

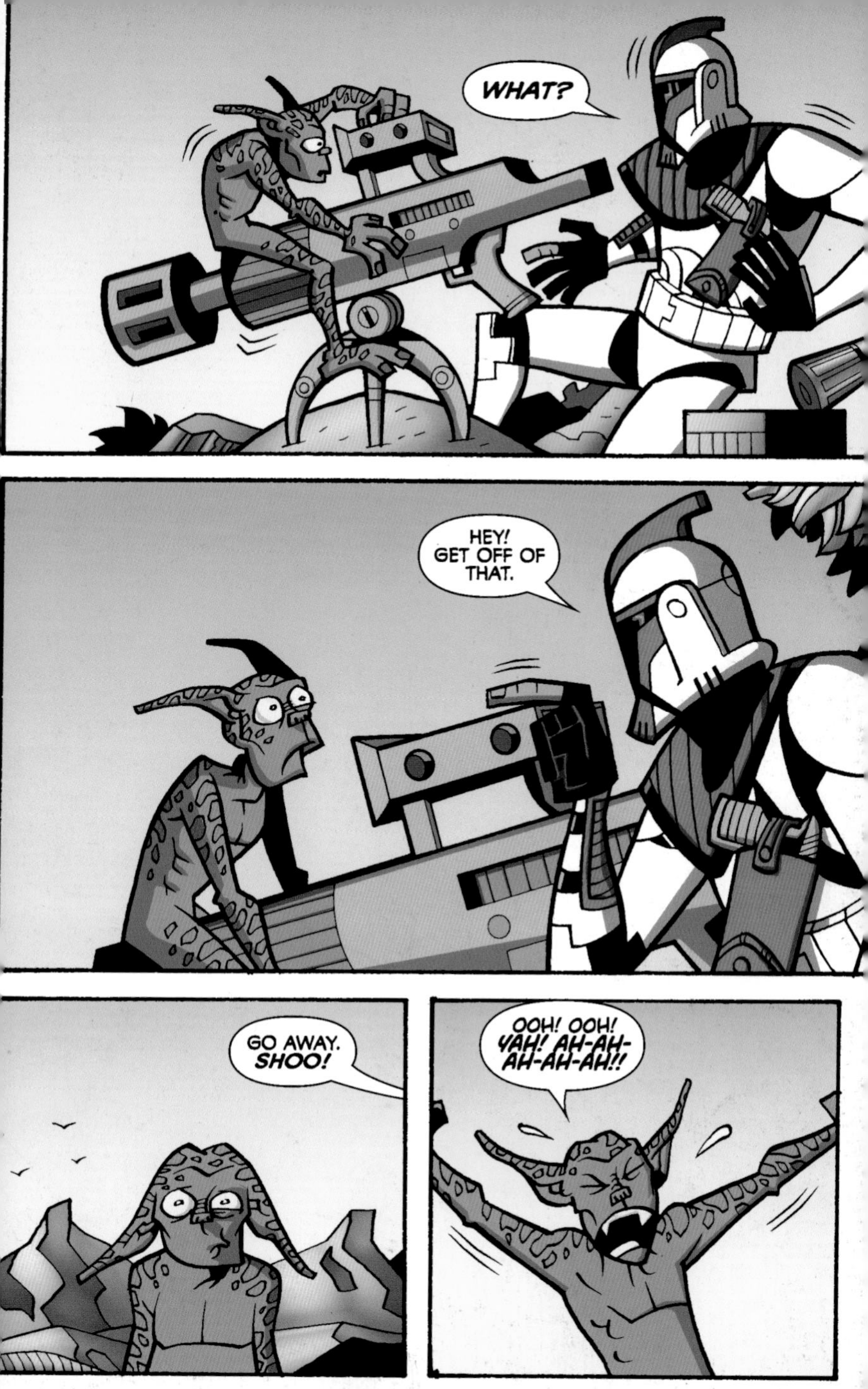
WHAT?
HEY! GET OFF OF THAT.
GO AWAY. SHOO!
OOH! OOH! YAH! AH-AH-AH-AH-AH!!

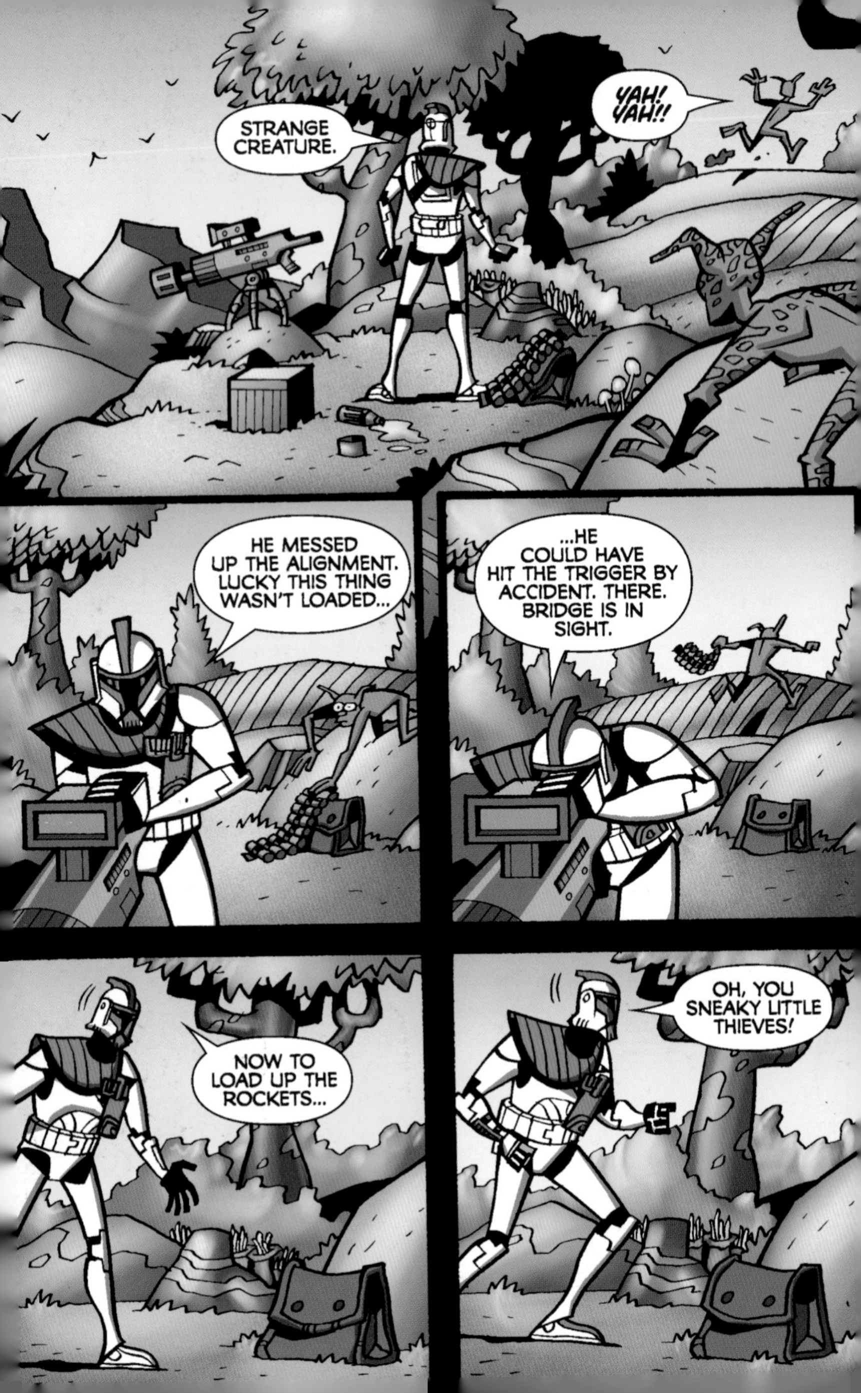
STRANGE CREATURE.
YAH! YAH!!
HE MESSED UP THE ALIGNMENT. LUCKY THIS THING WASN'T LOADED...
...HE COULD HAVE HIT THE TRIGGER BY ACCIDENT. THERE. BRIDGE IS IN SIGHT.
NOW TO LOAD UP THE ROCKETS...
OH, YOU SNEAKY LITTLE THIEVES!

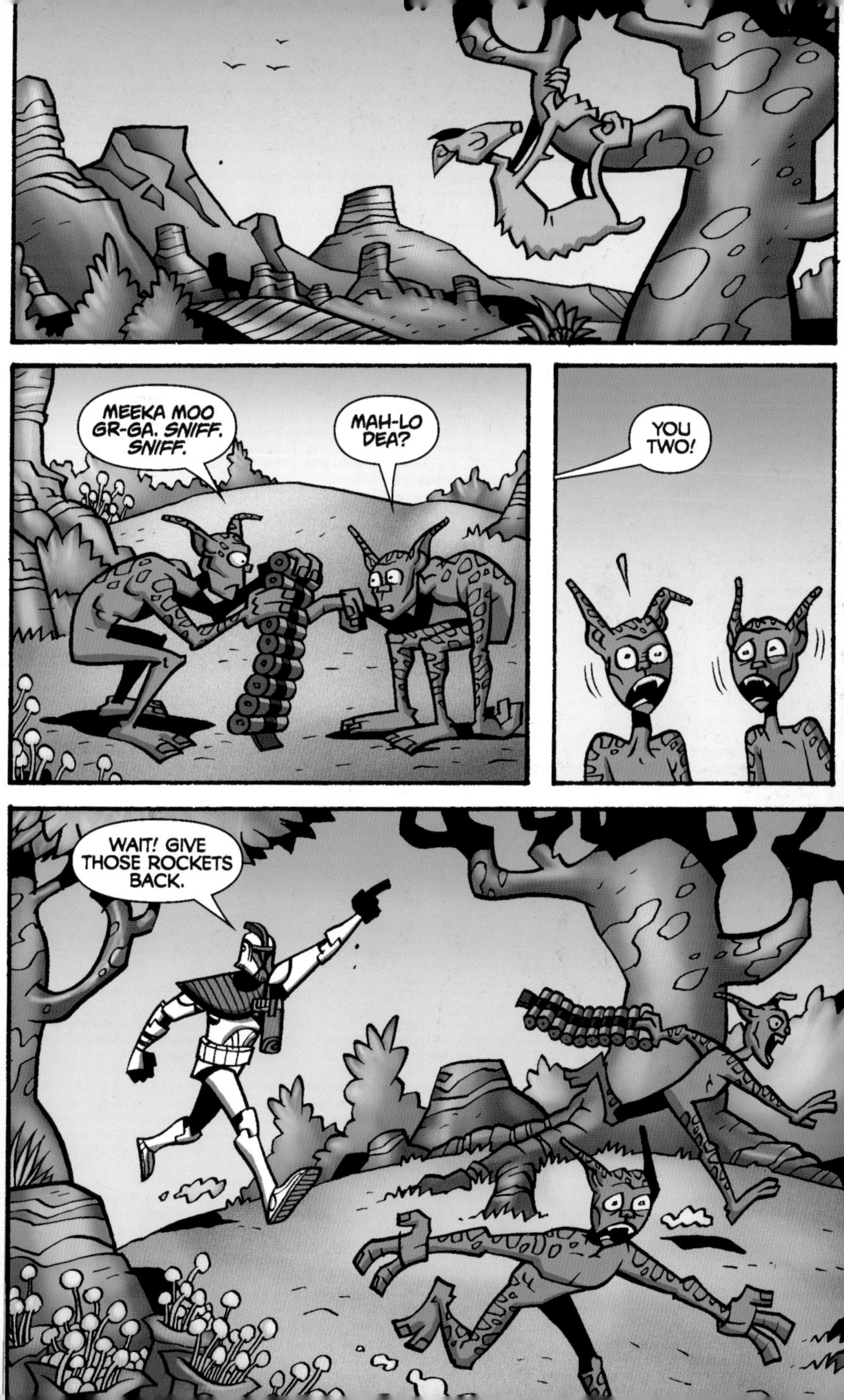
MEEKA MOO GR-GA. SNIFF. SNIFF.
MAH-LO DEA?
YOU TWO!
WAIT! GIVE THOSE ROCKETS BACK.

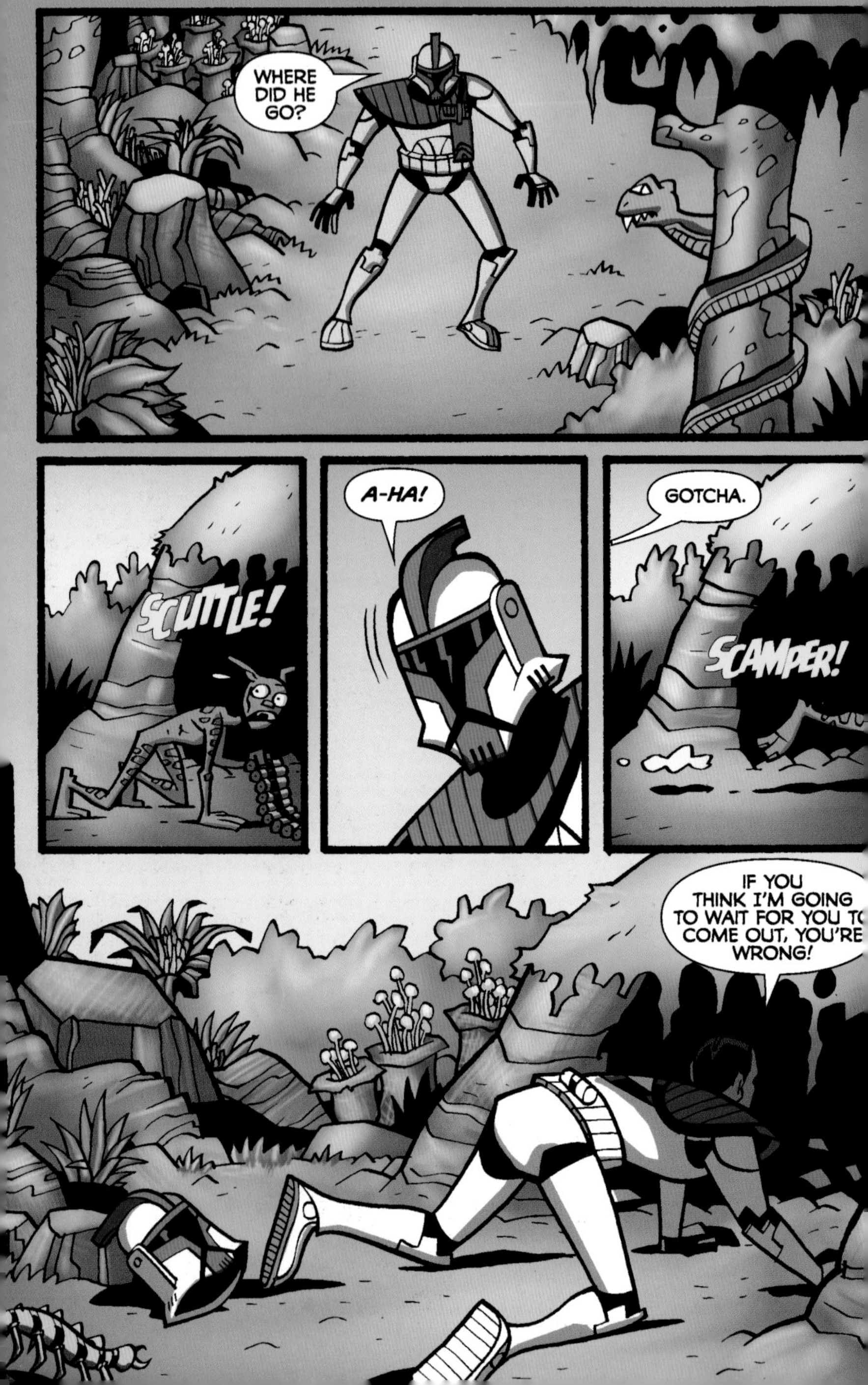
WHERE DID HE GO?
SCUTTLE!
A-HA!
GOTCHA.
SCAMPER!
IF YOU THINK I'M GOING TO WAIT FOR YOU TO COME OUT, YOU'RE WRONG!

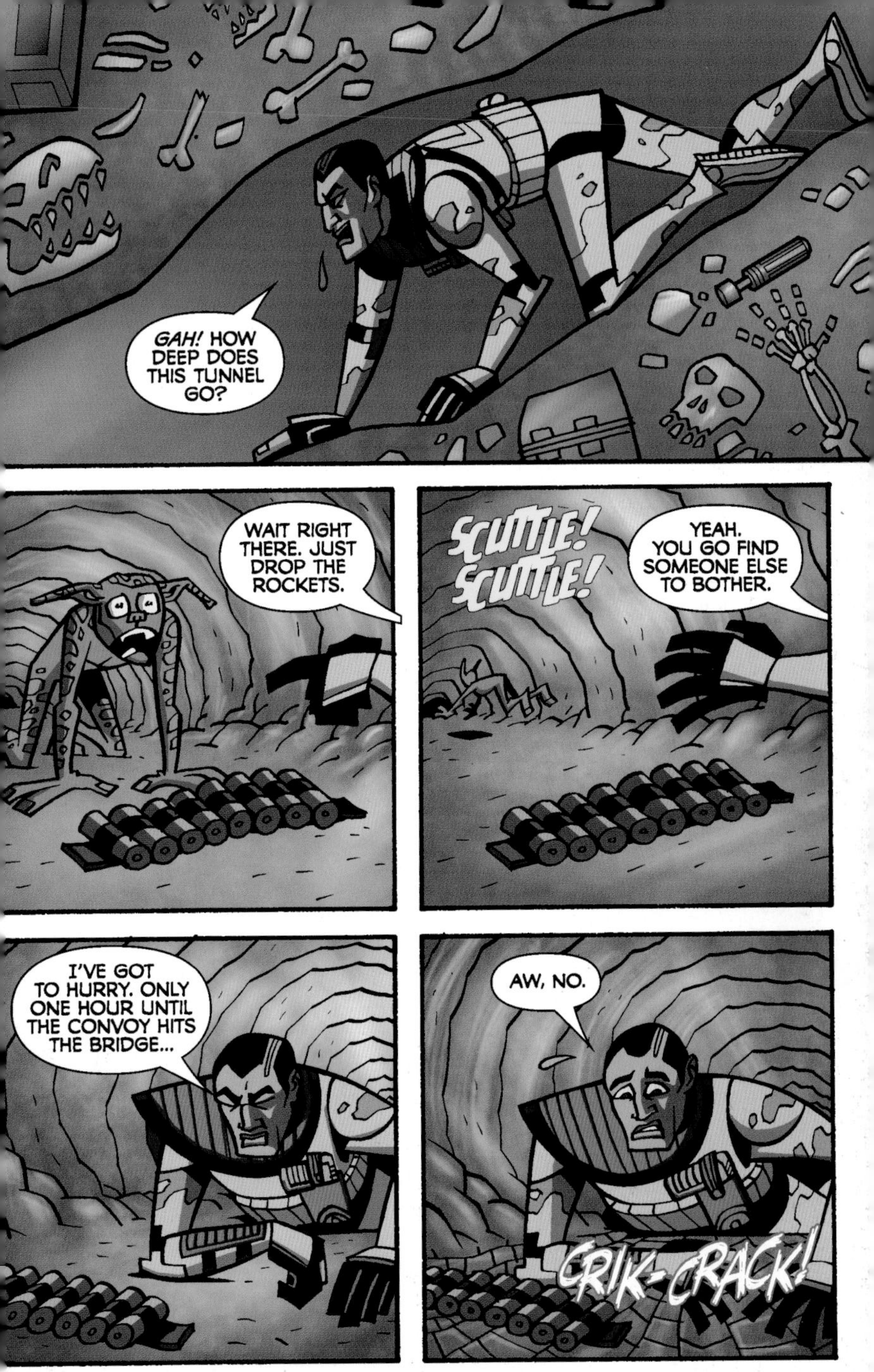
GAH! HOW DEEP DOES THIS TUNNEL GO?
WAIT RIGHT THERE. JUST DROP THE ROCKETS.
SCUTTLE! SCUTTLE!
YEAH. YOU GO FIND SOMEONE ELSE TO BOTHER.
I'VE GOT TO HURRY. ONLY ONE HOUR UNTIL THE CONVOY HITS THE BRIDGE...
AW, NO.
CRIK-CRACK!

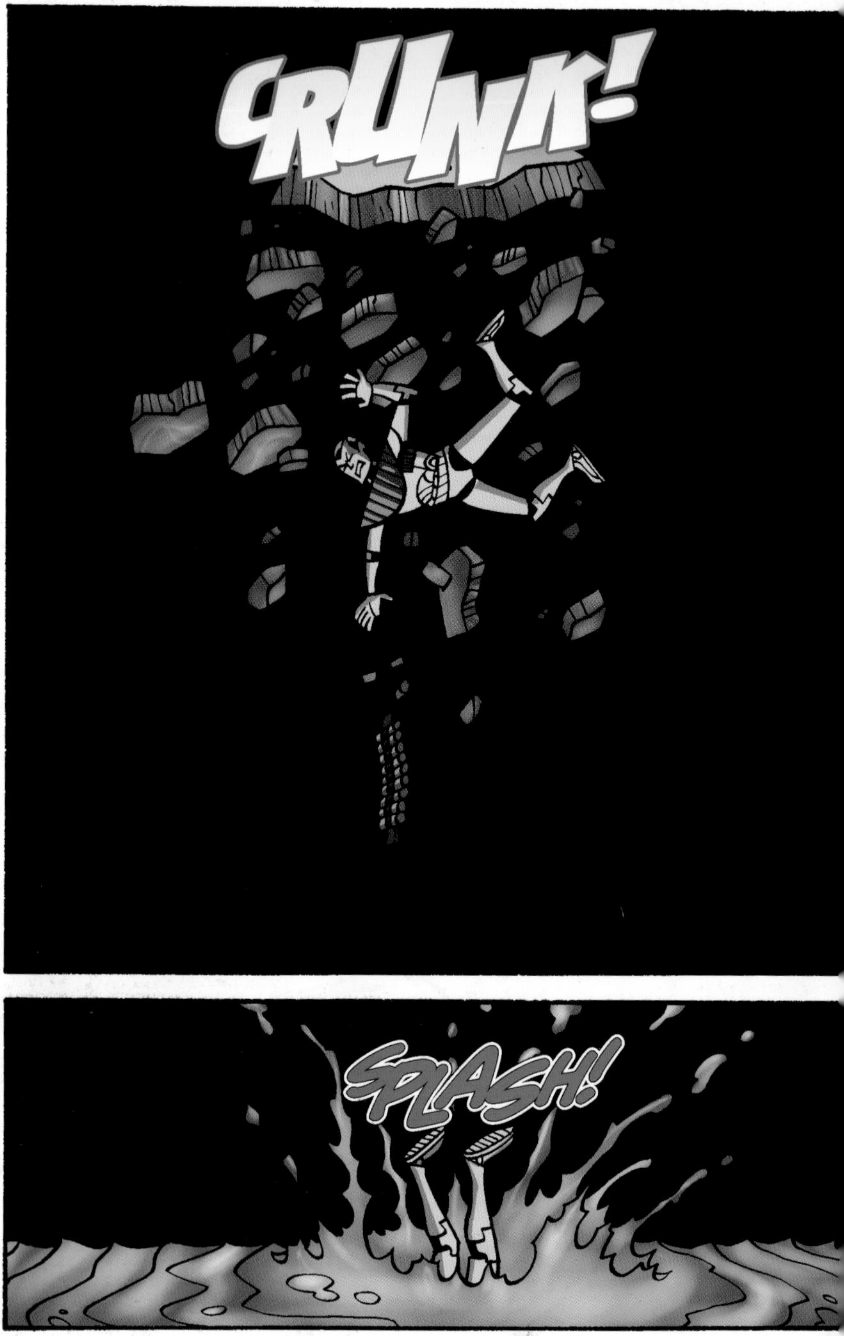
CRUNK!
SPLASH!

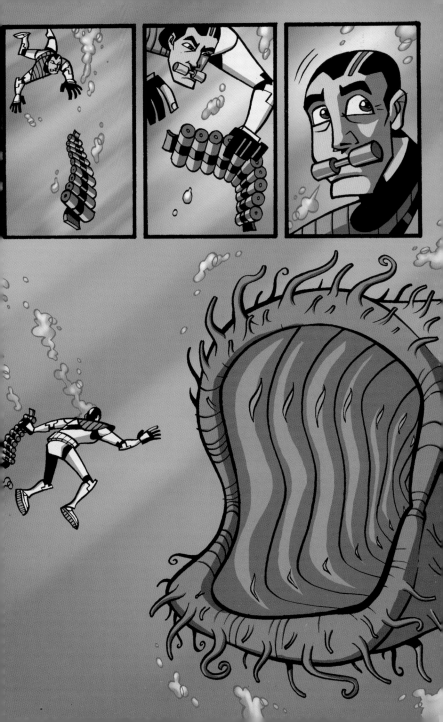

GULP!!

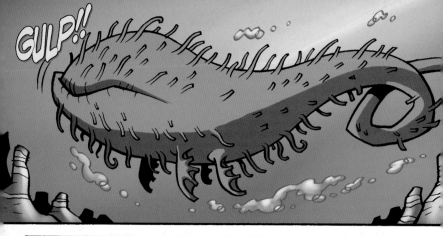

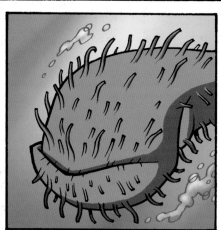

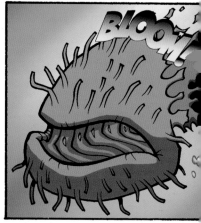

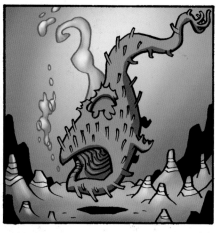

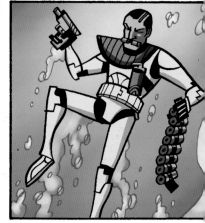

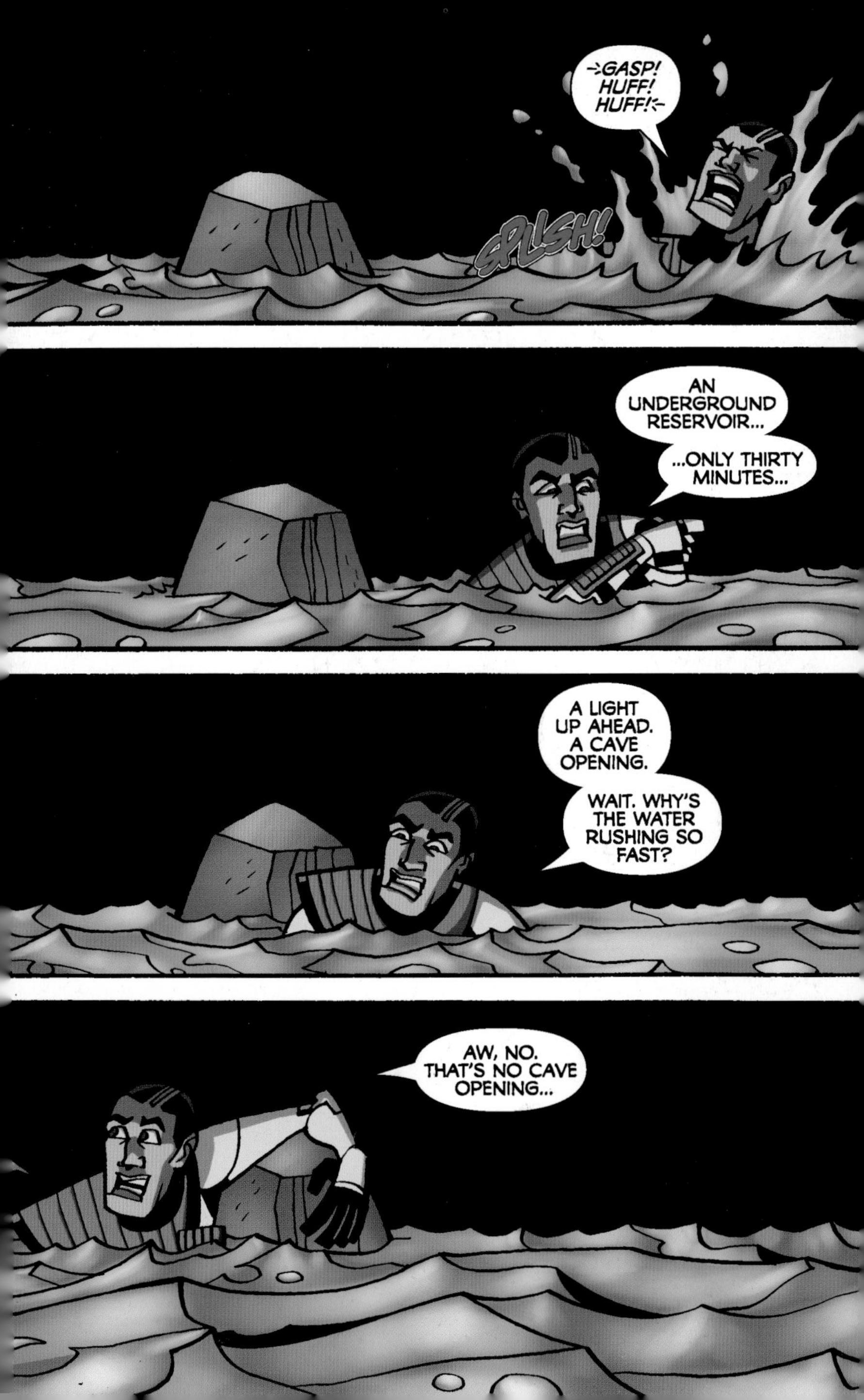
GASP! HUFF! HUFF!
SPLISH!
AN UNDERGROUND RESERVOIR...
...ONLY THIRTY MINUTES...
A LIGHT UP AHEAD. A CAVE OPENING.
WAIT. WHY'S THE WATER RUSHING SO FAST?
AW, NO. THAT'S NO CAVE OPENING...

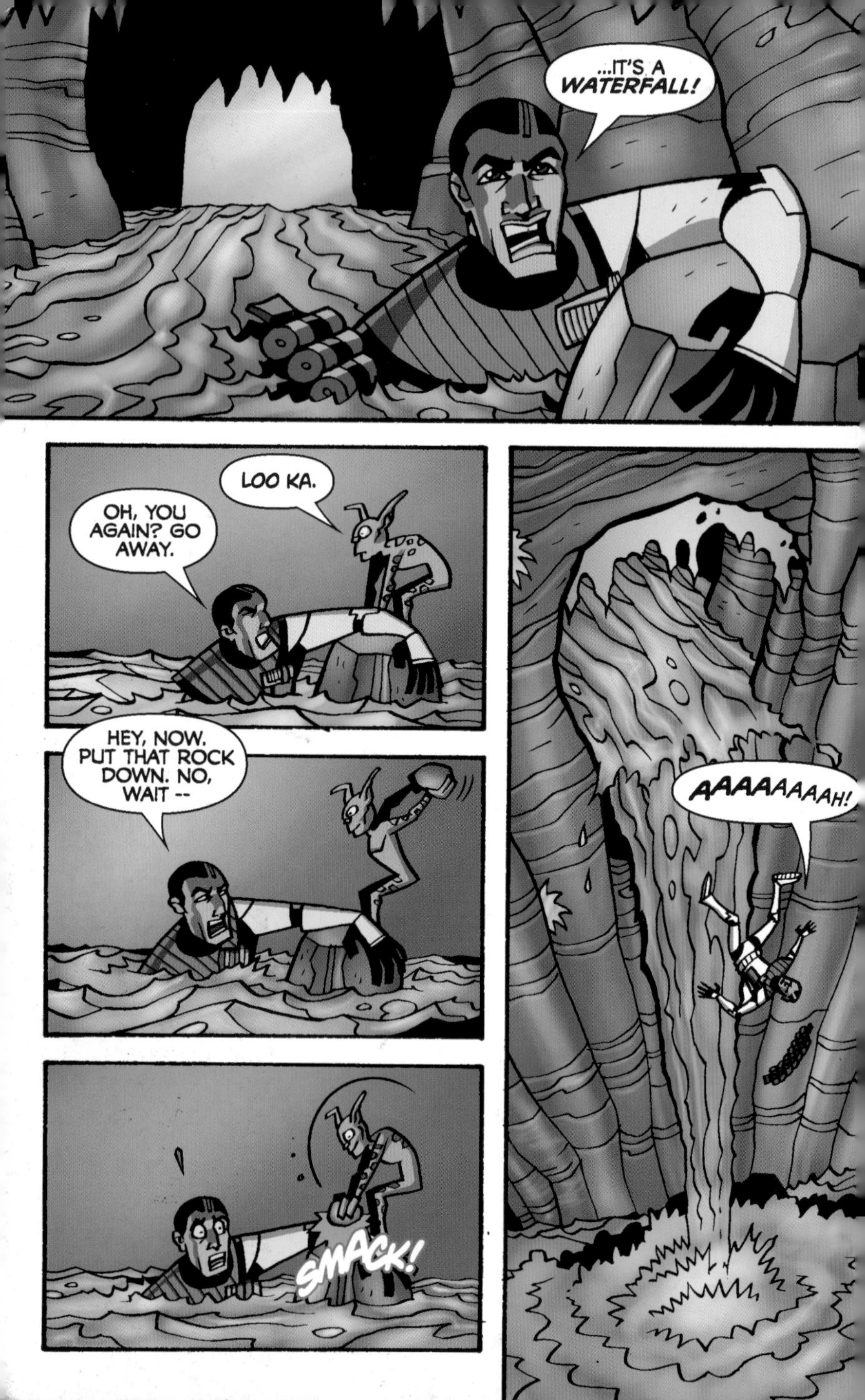
...IT'S A WATERFALL!
LOO KA.
OH, YOU AGAIN? GO AWAY.
HEY, NOW. PUT THAT ROCK DOWN. NO, WAIT --
SMACK!
AAAAAAAAH!

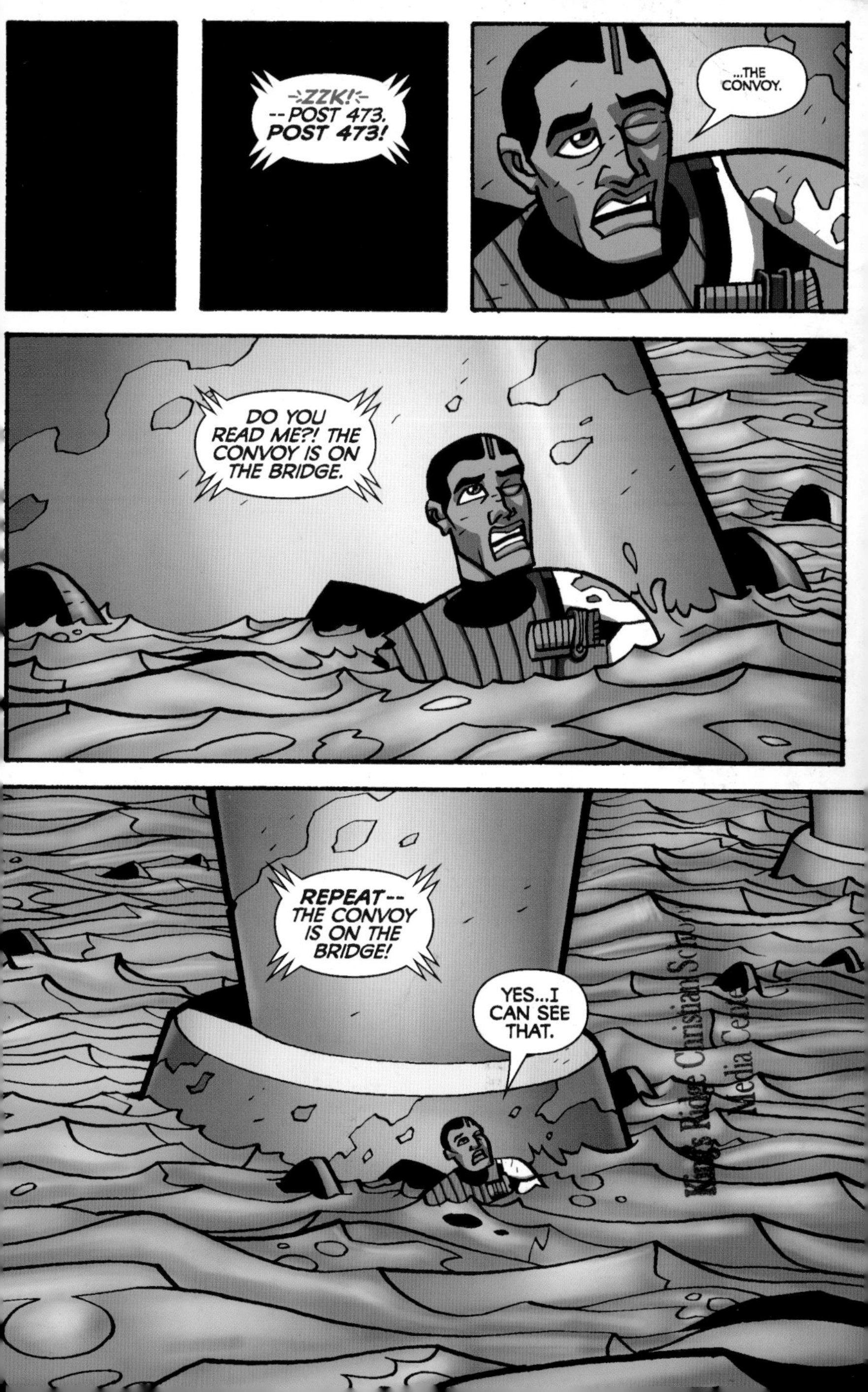
-ZZK!- --POST 473. POST 473!
...THE CONVOY.
DO YOU READ ME?! THE CONVOY IS ON THE BRIDGE.
REPEAT-- THE CONVOY IS ON THE BRIDGE!
YES...I CAN SEE THAT.

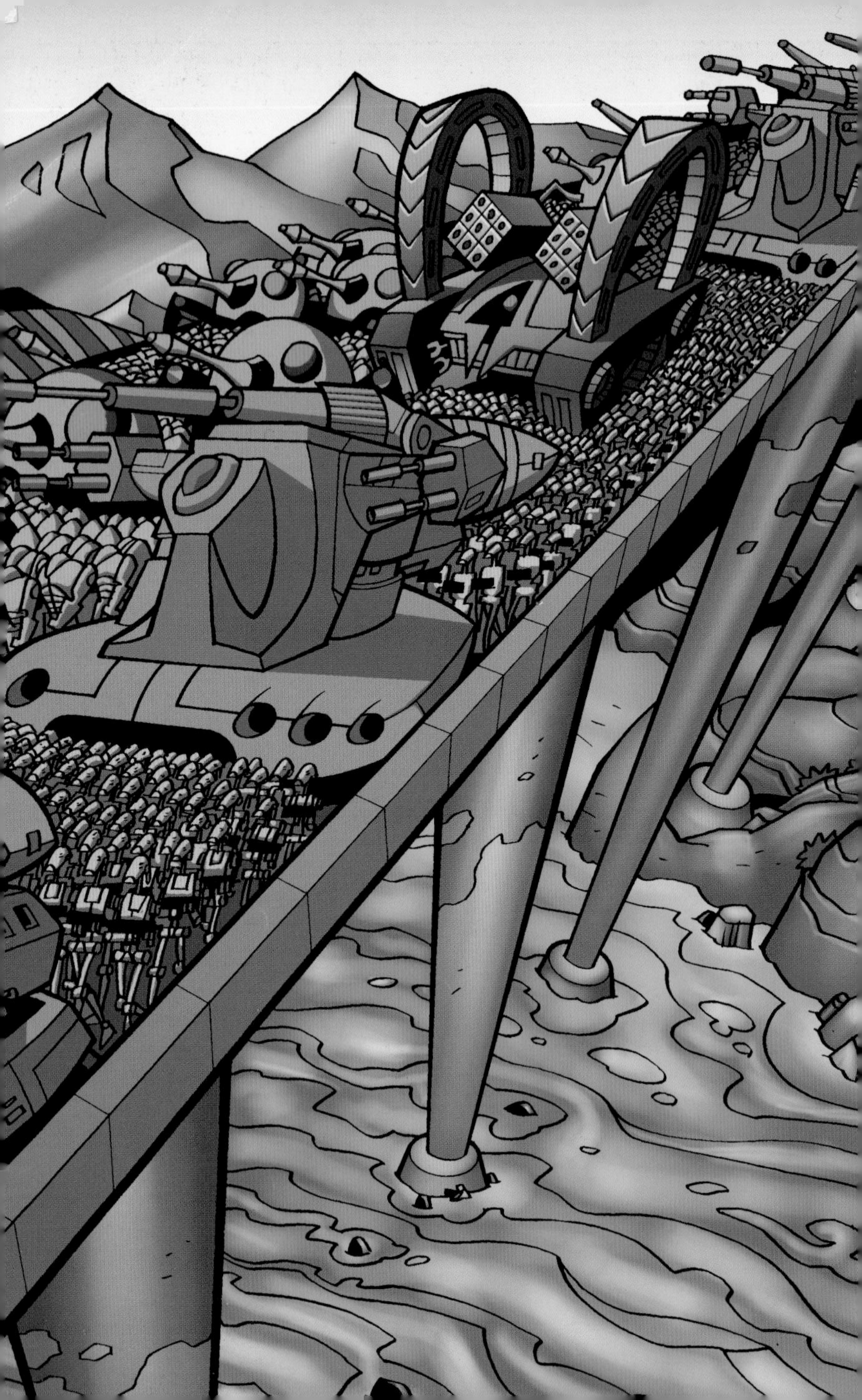

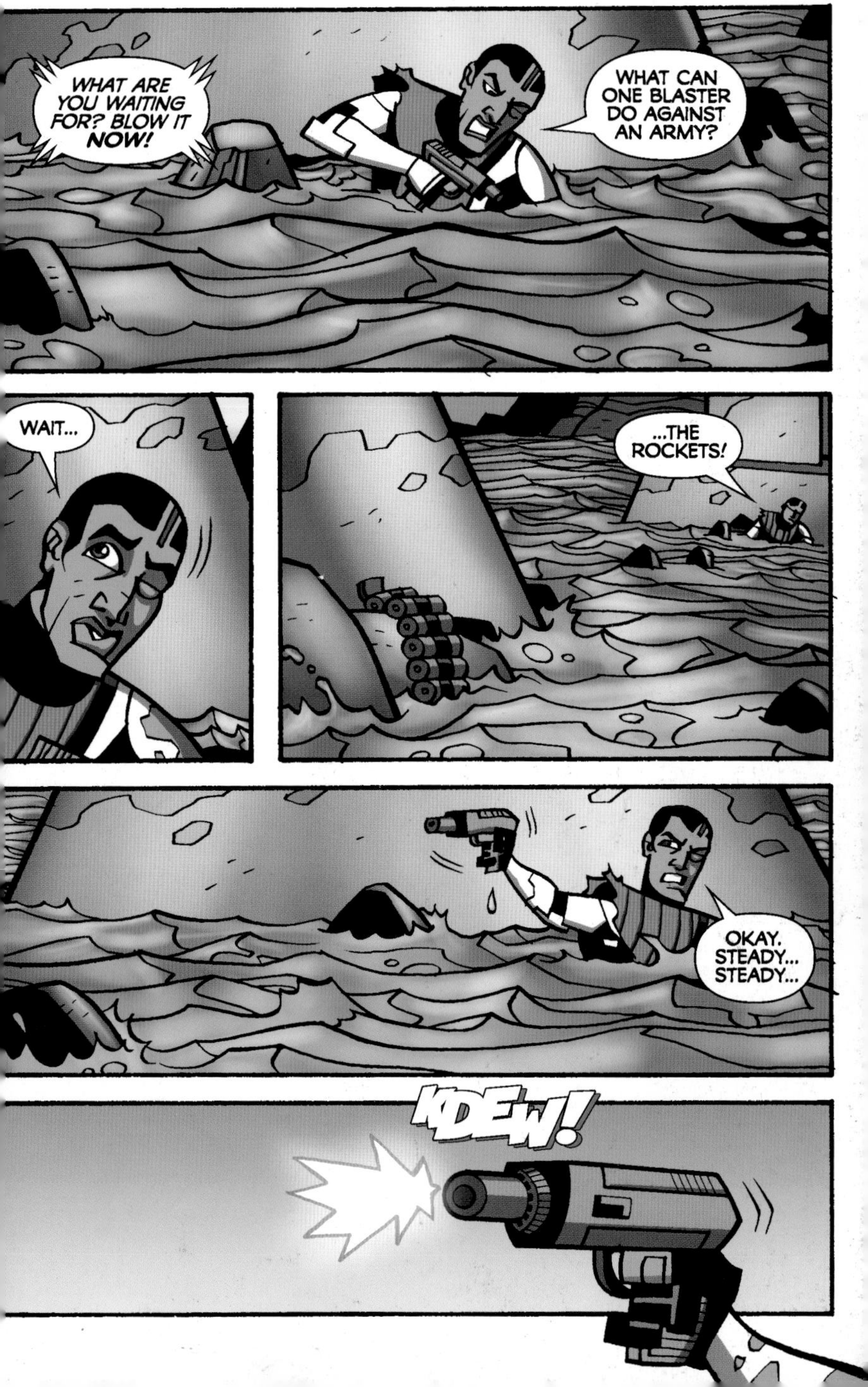
WHAT ARE YOU WAITING FOR? BLOW IT NOW!
WHAT CAN ONE BLASTER DO AGAINST AN ARMY?
WAIT...
...THE ROCKETS!
OKAY. STEADY... STEADY...
KDEW!

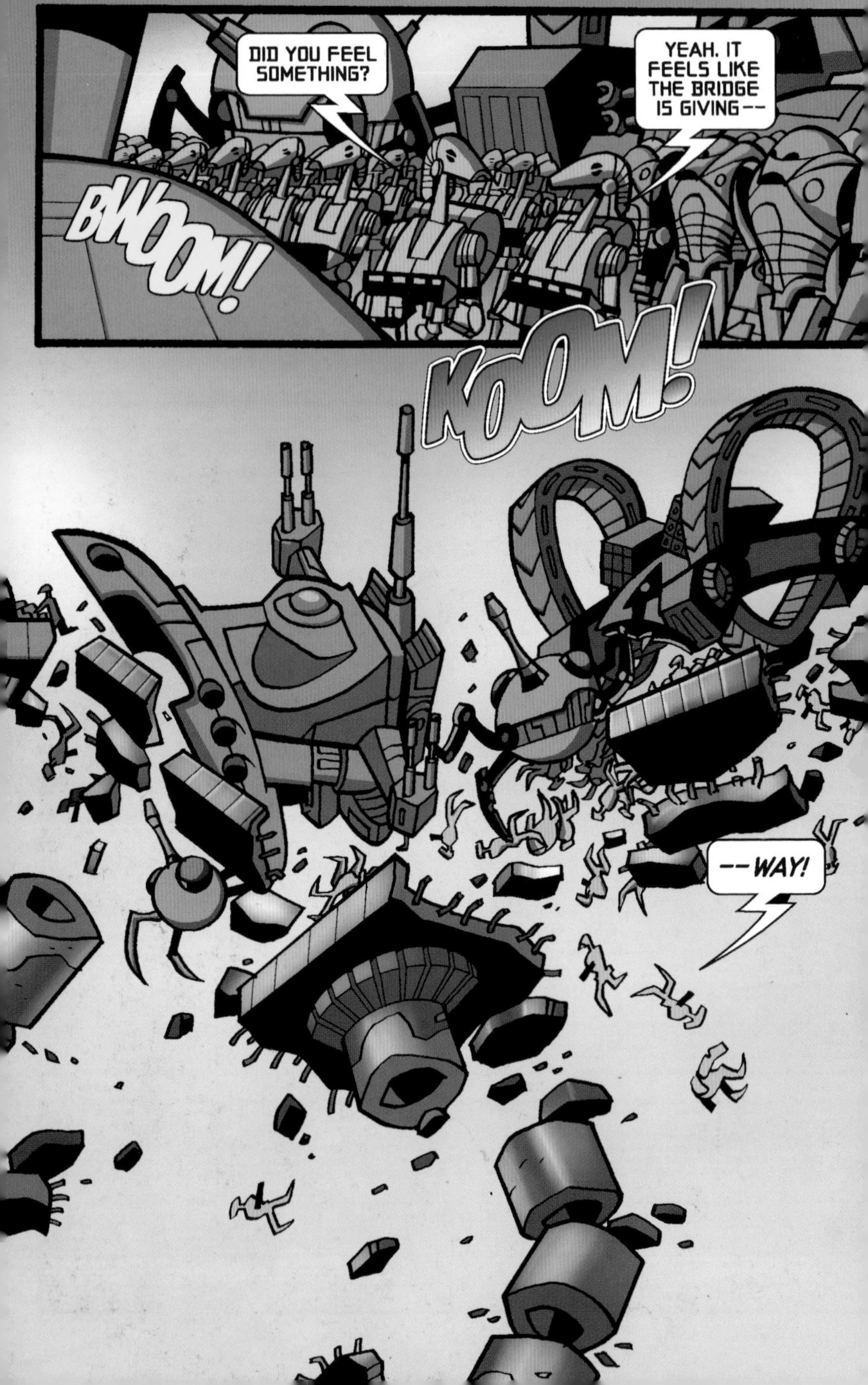
DID YOU FEEL SOMETHING?
YEAH. IT FEELS LIKE THE BRIDGE IS GIVING--
BWOOM!
KOOM!
--WAY!

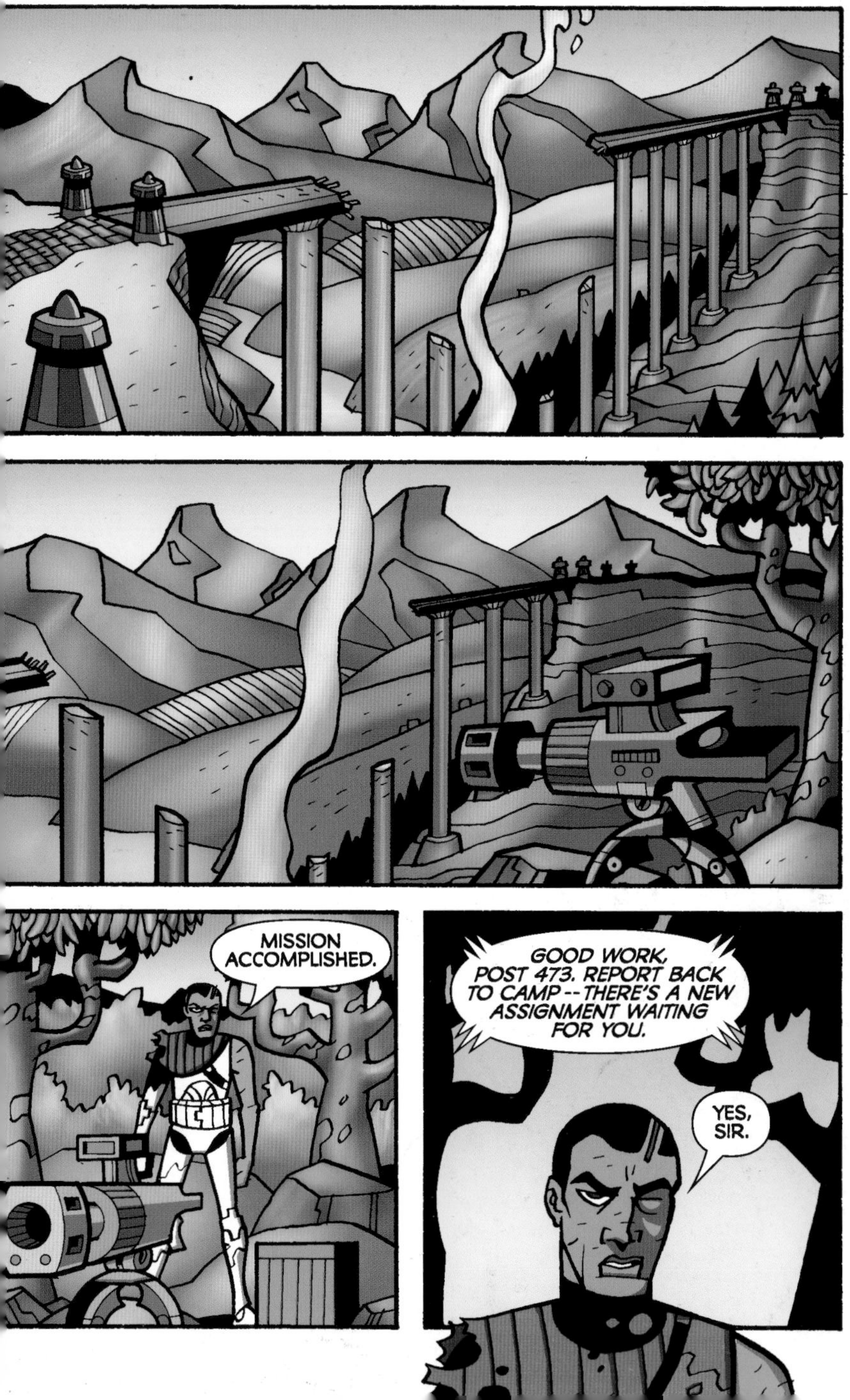
MISSION ACCOMPLISHED.
GOOD WORK, POST 473. REPORT BACK TO CAMP--THERE'S A NEW ASSIGNMENT WAITING FOR YOU.
YES, SIR.

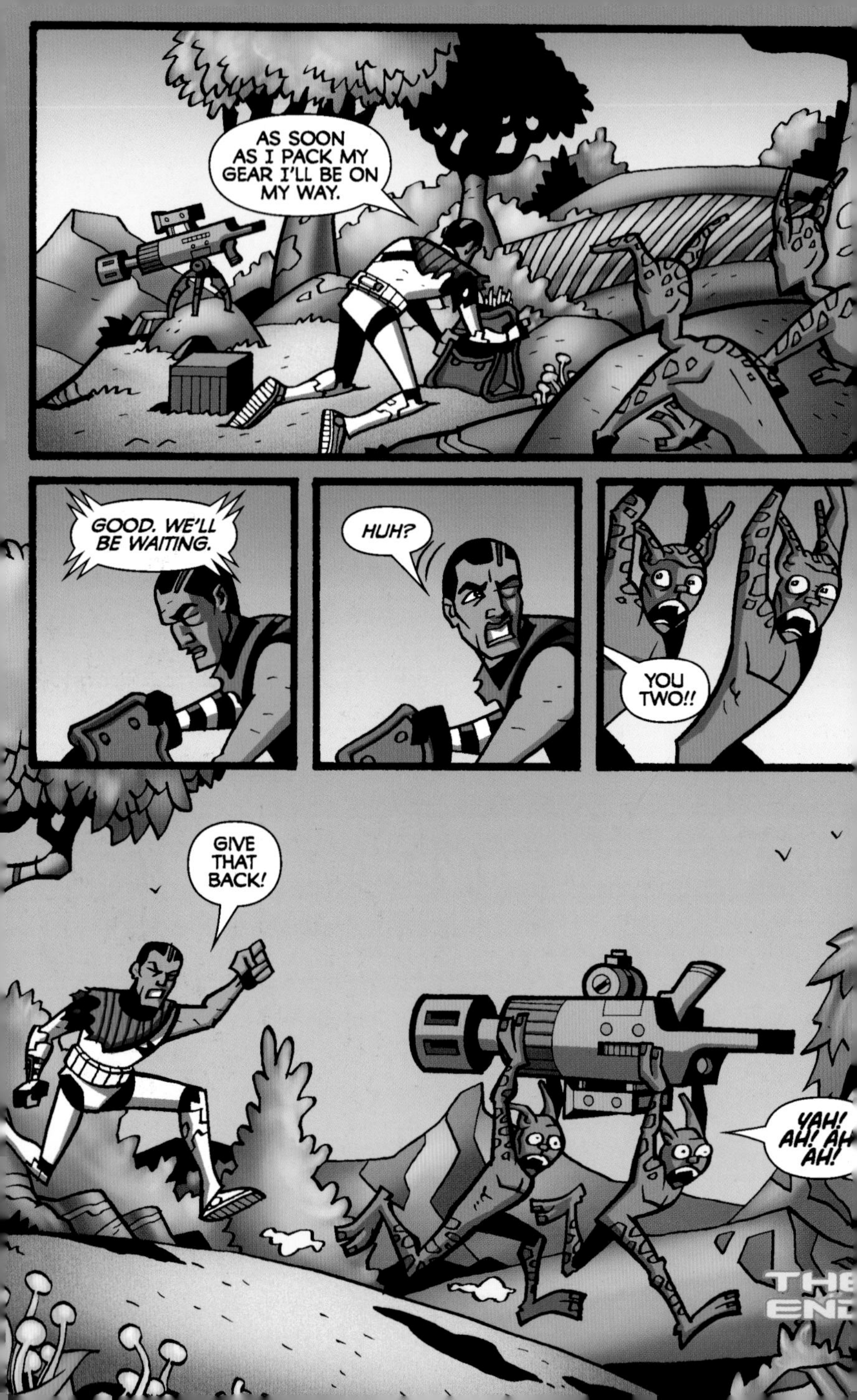
AS SOON AS I PACK MY GEAR I'LL BE ON MY WAY.
GOOD. WE'LL BE WAITING.
HUH?
YOU TWO!!
GIVE THAT BACK!
YAH! AH! AH! AH!
THE END

STAR WARS®
CLONE WARS ADVENTURES

Don't miss any of the action-packed adventures of your favorite STAR WARS® characters, available at comics shops and bookstores in a galaxy near you!

STAR WARS
CLONE WARS ADVENTURES

Volume 1
SBN-10: 1-59307-243-0
N-13: 978-1-59307-243-8

STAR WARS
CLONE WARS ADVENTURES
THREE TALES OF HYPERKINETIC JEDI ACTION!

Volume 2
ISBN-10: 1-59307-271-6
ISBN-13: 978-1-59307-271-1

STAR WARS
CLONE WARS ADVENTURES
FOUR TALES OF SINISTER SEPARATIST SCHEMING AND ROCKING REPUBLIC COMBAT!

Volume 3
ISBN-10: 1-59307-307-0
ISBN-13: 978-1-59307-307-7

STAR WARS
CLONE WARS ADVENTURES
FOUR RIVETING ADVENTURES IN ONE FANTASTIC VOLUME!

Volume 4
ISBN-10: 1-59307-402-6
ISBN-13: 978-1-59307-402-9

STAR WARS
CLONE WARS ADVENTURES

Volume 5
SBN-10: 1-59307-483-2
N-13: 978-1-59307-483-8

STAR WARS
CLONE WARS ADVENTURES
FOUR TALES OF PLANETS IN PERIL AND JEDI IN JEOPARDY!

Volume 6
ISBN-10: 1-59307-567-7
ISBN-13: 978-1-59307-567-5

STAR WARS
CLONE WARS ADVENTURES

Volume 7
ISBN-10: 1-59307-678-9
ISBN-13: 978-1-59307-678-8

STAR WARS
CLONE WARS ADVENTURES

Volume 8
ISBN-10: 1-59307-680-0
ISBN-13: 978-1-59307-680-1
Coming in June!

$6.95 each!

To find a comics shop in your area, call 1-888-266-4226
or more information or to order direct: • On the web: darkhorse.com • Phone: 1-800-862-0052 Mon.-Fri. 9 A.M. to 5 P.M. Pacific Time.
• E-mail: mailorder@darkhorse.com *Prices and availability subject to change without notice.

STAR WARS®
CLONE WARS

Experience all the excitement and drama of the Clone Wars! Look for these trade paperbacks at a comics shop or book store near you!

VOLUME 1: THE DEFENSE OF KAMINO
ISBN-10: 1-56971-962-4
ISBN-13: 978-1-56971-962-6
$14.95

VOLUME 2: VICTORIES AND SACRIFICES
ISBN-10: 1-56971-969-1
ISBN-13: 978-1-56971-969-5
$14.95

VOLUME 3: LAST STAND ON JABIIM
ISBN-10: 1-59307-006-3
ISBN-13: 978-1-59307-006-9
$14.95

VOLUME 4: LIGHT AND DARK
ISBN-10: 1-59307-195-7
ISBN-13: 978-1-59307-195-0
$16.95

VOLUME 5: THE BEST BLADES
ISBN-10: 1-59307-273-2
ISBN-13: 978-1-59307-273-5
$14.95

VOLUME 6: ON THE FIELDS OF BATTLE
ISBN-10: 1-59307-352-6
ISBN-13: 978-1-59307-352-7
$17.95

VOLUME 7: WHEN THEY WERE BROTHERS
ISBN-10: 1-59307-396-8
ISBN-13: 978-1-59307-396-1
$17.95

VOLUME 8: THE LAST SIEGE, THE FINAL TRUTH
ISBN-10: 1-59307-482-4
ISBN-13: 978-1-59307-482-1
$17.95

VOLUME 9: ENDGAME
ISBN-10: 1-59307-553-7
ISBN-13: 978-1-59307-553-8
$17.95

To find a comics shop in your area, call 1-888-266-4226
For more information or to order direct:
- On the web: darkhorse.com
- E-mail: mailorder@darkhorse.com
- Phone: 1-800-862-0052

Mon.-Fri. 9 A.M. to 5 P.M. Pacific Time
*Prices and availability subject to change without notice.

READY TO TRY SOME OTHER GREAT STAR WARS® TITLES?

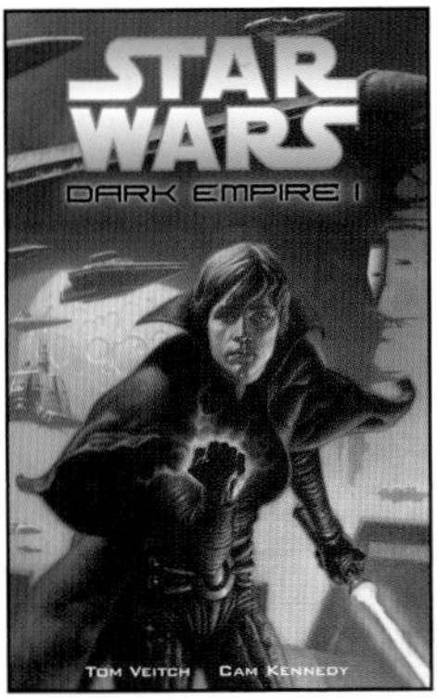
STAR WARS
DARK EMPIRE I
TOM VEITCH CAM KENNEDY

DARK EMPIRE

n Luke, Leia, Han, and Chewie as they battle the ipire's latest super-weapons: the gigantic, planet-stroying World Devastators!

SBN-10: 1-59307-039-X / ISBN-13: 978-1-59307-039-7

$16.95

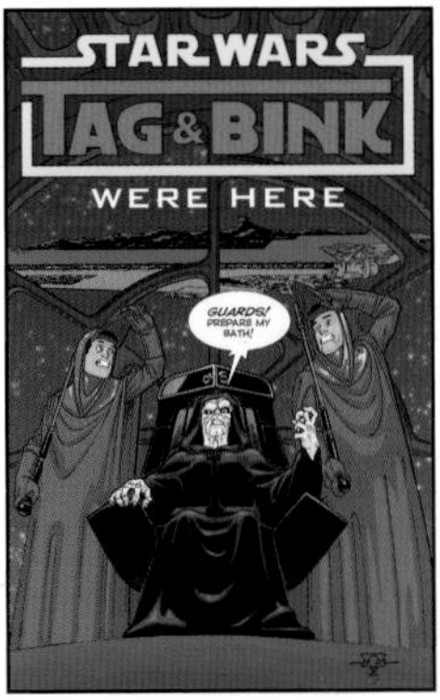
STAR WARS
TAG & BINK
WERE HERE
GUARDS! PREPARE MY BATH!

TAG AND BINK WERE HERE

Laugh yourself into orbit with the hilarious misadventures of a pair of hapless Rebel officers!

ISBN-10: 1-59307-641-X / ISBN-13: 978-1-59307-641-2

$14.95

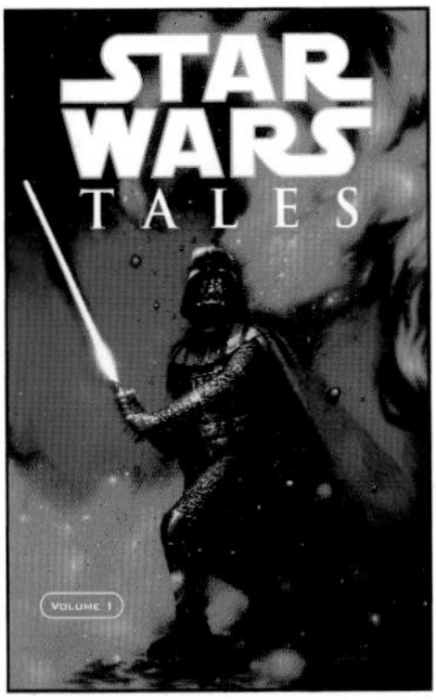
STAR WARS
TALES
VOLUME I

TALES VOLUME 1

ad the first four issues of the quarterly anthology ash sensation that explores every corner of the *Star rs* galaxy!

SBN-10: 1-56971-619-6 / ISBN-13: 978-1-56971-619-9

$19.95

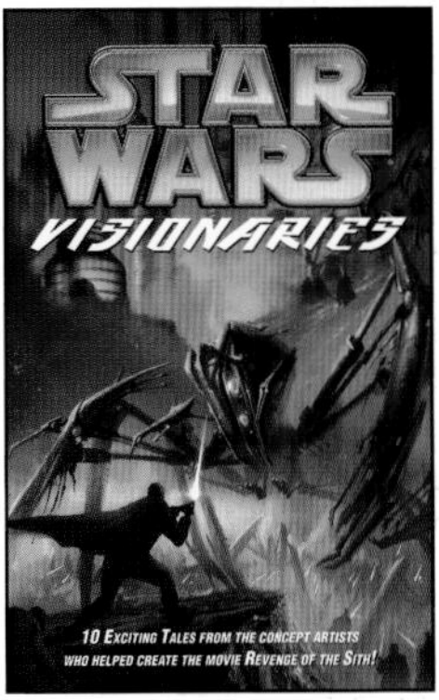
STAR WARS
VISIONARIES
10 EXCITING TALES FROM THE CONCEPT ARTISTS
WHO HELPED CREATE THE MOVIE REVENGE OF THE SITH!

VISIONARIES

Ten exciting tales from the concept artists who helped create the movie *Revenge of the Sith*!

ISBN-10: 1-59307-311-9 / ISBN-13: 978-1-59307-311-4

$17.95

DARK HORSE BOOKS

AVAILABLE AT YOUR LOCAL COMICS SHOP OR BOOKSTORE!

To find a comics shop in your area, call 1-888-266-4226

For more information or to order direct visit darkhorse.com or call 1-800-862-0052 Mon.-Fri. 9 A.M. to 5 P.M. Pacific Time.

Prices and availability subject to change without notice.

STAR WARS GRAPHIC NOVEL TIMELINE (IN YEAR

Tales of the Jedi—5,000–3,986 BSW4
Knights of the Old Republic—3,964 BSW4
Jedi vs. Sith—1,000 BSW4
Jedi Council: Acts of War—33 BSW4
Prelude to Rebellion—33 BSW4
Darth Maul—33 BSW4
Episode I: The Phantom Menace—32 BSW4
Outlander—32 BSW4
Emissaries to Malastare—32 BSW4
Jango Fett: Open Seasons—32 BSW4
Twilight—31 BSW4
Bounty Hunters—31 BSW4
The Hunt for Aurra Sing—30 BSW4
Darkness—30 BSW4
The Stark Hyperspace War—30 BSW4
Rite of Passage—28 BSW4
Jango Fett—27 BSW4
Zam Wesell—27 BSW4
Honor and Duty—24 BSW4
Episode II: Attack of the Clones—22 BSW4
Clone Wars—22–19 BSW4
Clone Wars Adventures—22–19 BSW4
General Grievous—20 BSW4
Episode III: Revenge of the Sith—19 BSW4
Dark Times—19 BSW4
Droids—3 BSW4
Boba Fett: Enemy of the Empire—2 BSW4
Underworld—1 BSW4
Episode IV: A New Hope—SW4
Classic Star Wars—0–3 ASW4
A Long Time Ago . . .—0–4 ASW4
Empire—0 ASW4
Rebellion—0 ASW4
Vader's Quest—0 ASW4
Boba Fett: Man with a Mission—0 ASW4
Jabba the Hutt: The Art of the Deal—1 ASW4
Splinter of the Mind's Eye—1 ASW4
Episode V: The Empire Strikes Back—3 ASW4
Shadows of the Empire—3–5 ASW4
Episode VI: Return of the Jedi—4 ASW4
X-Wing Rogue Squadron—4–5 ASW4
Mara Jade: By the Emperor's Hand—4 ASW4
Heir to the Empire—9 ASW4
Dark Force Rising—9 ASW4
The Last Command—9 ASW4
Dark Empire—10 ASW4
Boba Fett: Death, Lies, and Treachery—11 ASW4
Crimson Empire—11 ASW4
Jedi Academy: Leviathan—13 ASW4
Union—20 ASW4
Chewbacca—25 ASW4
Legacy—130 ASW4

Old Republic Era
25,000 – 1000 years before
Star Wars: A New Hope

Rise of the Empire Era
1000 – 0 years before
Star Wars: A New Hope

Rebellion Era
0 – 5 years after
Star Wars: A New Hope

New Republic Era
5 – 25 years after
Star Wars: A New Hope

New Jedi Order Era
25+ years after
Star Wars: A New Hope

Legacy Era
130+ years after
Star Wars: A New Hope

Infinities
Does not apply to timeline

Sergio Aragonés Stomps Star Wars
Star Wars Tales
Star Wars Infinities
Tag and Bink
Star Wars Visionaries

BSW4 = before *Episode IV: A New Hope*. ASW4 = after *Episode IV: A New Hope*.